Ennobling Encounters

Richard J. Bishirjian

En Route Books and Media, LLC

Saint Louis, MO

⊕ENROUTE
Make the time

En Route Books and Media, LLC
5705 Rhodes Avenue
St. Louis, MO 63109

Cover Design: Avery Easter

Copyright © 2021
American Academy of Distance Learning, Inc.

ISBN-13: 978-1-952464-90-4
Library of Congress Control Number: 2021942953

Contents

Acknowledgment

Publication of *Ennobling Encounters* is made possible by the gracious support of Wayne Valis, a deep admirer of Vic Milione and Gerhart Niemeyer.

Introduction

My life has been enriched by many noble persons, and this book introduces you to those whom I met during my professional life. That time coincides with the early years of the Conservative Movement in America.

I had become a political conservative when I was an undergraduate student at the University of Pittsburgh and worked part time in Republican Party HQ in Allegheny County during the Fall of 1960. My growing knowledge of conservative ideas led to my encounter with émigré philosophers at the University of Notre Dame, where in January of 1965, I was admitted to graduate study in the Department of Government.

The time was twenty years after World War II, and I did not know what these men would teach me. But I was twenty-two years old in 1964, and I had made a commitment to view life, politics, and history from the perspective of an American political conservative. This is a story about men who ennobled me and is my attempt to honor them.

††††

When I was born, World War II was being fought in Europe and the Pacific, and my father was with the 3rd

Marine Division where he saw fighting at Iwo Jima and Saipan. Consequently, I didn't meet him until he returned from the war. Had we invaded Japan, most likely I would never have known him.

I was three years old and was living with my mother on the second floor of a private home in Wilkinsburg, a suburb of Pittsburgh, Pennsylvania. I was spoiled rotten, and my first memory of my father was when he put a stop to my acting out when I fussed over my food.

From my birth until I entered the University of Pittsburgh as a freshman, except for two years when my parents moved to Miami, Florida, I lived my entire life in the "Burg," as Pittsburgh is affectionately called.

Pittsburgh was then a symphony of ethnic communities that included Lawrenceville (Polish), the Hill District (African American), Squirrel Hill (Jewish), Oakland and Mt. Lebanon (WASP), and other areas occupied by Germans, Irish, and Italians. The largest ethnic group was—and still is—German. My mother's father was an ethnic German, his eldest children spoke German, our family attended a German Lutheran Church, and I attended a Lutheran grade school.

In Pittsburgh, my life centered on my Lutheran church. Apart from an uncle's wedding to a Catholic, the first time I entered a Catholic Church, St. Paul's in Oakland, situated a few blocks from the campus of the University of Pittsburgh, was on the day President John F. Kennedy was assassinated.

Second in importance in my life were the Pittsburgh Pirates who played at Forbes Field, located across from Pitt's Cathedral of Learning, where in summer I sold newspapers.

I loved my life as a Pittsburgher, and to this day I enjoy returning "home" to the Burg and memories of past experience.

At the end of my freshman year at the University of Pittsburgh in June, 1961, I worked on "political referral" by Rep. Robert J. Corbett (R-PA) as a GS-3 Clerk typist at the General Services Administration in Washington, D.C., in the office of George Gryc in the U.S. Geological Survey. The presidential election of 1960 had confirmed my commitment to the conservative movement, and I wrote to *Human Events*, a conservative American political news and analysis newspaper, offering my services in any way I was needed. W. B. Hicks called my aunt's home where I was staying that summer and invited me to become an intern.

After work, I would go to the offices of *Human Events* on Capitol Hill and join a handful of young conservatives where M. Stanton Evans would give talks about American government. That summer, *Human Events* conducted its first Political Action Conference and Henry Regnery invited me to work in his Regnery Publishing Company booth. Just this past year, I purchased Henry Regnery's *Memoirs of a Dissident Publisher* and read these words about one of his authors, Max Picard, a medical doctor, who had written *The Human Face* (1929) and *The Flight from God* (1934). Like his friend Gabriel Marcel, Picard was a self-professed "neo-Socratic":

> *Picard felt strongly that one of the things lacking in modern life is the true encounter—people see and talk to each other but do not really encounter one another; the one gives nothing of himself to the other.*

Those words motivated me to write this book and to share my thoughts about the noble persons I have encountered in the belief that the few noble souls we encounter in life are definitive in shaping our souls and thus our humanity.

The most important persons we meet in life, of course, are our parents. Surely, the accident of my birth in these United States—growing up in America when I did—was determinative in making me who I am and what I became.

Being born in 1942 to a mother and father who themselves were formed by the accident of their births, the heritage of their parents and grandparents and the difficult times they endured growing up during the Great Depression and World War II, shaped them and me.

My mother's father, my grandfather, Adolph Olen, was an ethnic German who emigrated before World War I to the United States from a small town about ten kilometers from Warsaw when Poland was part of Germany. His family name, Olensche, was Polish, but he was a German Lutheran, as was my mother.

My father's father and mother, who had grown up three houses down and across the street from one another in the East Liberty section of Pittsburgh, were Armenian immigrants. My grandfather, Hagop Bishirjian, left Aintab, Turkey, in 1912, three years before the Armenian genocide. My grandmother, Sarah Kevorkian, and her sisters fled Aleppo, Syria, to Egypt and experienced the hardships of those terrible times when Armenian Christians suffered a genocide at the hands of Turkish Muslims reeling from the loss of the Ottoman government that had allied with the Central Powers (namely, Germany, Austria-Hungary, the Ottoman Empire, and Bulgaria) in World War I.

That diaspora had brought great hardships to the Armenian community that escaped to the United States, and the few Armenian families living in Pittsburgh were too small in number to support an Armenian church. We, their children and grandchildren, became assimilated. I was raised a Lutheran and was shaped, as a result, by Western, not Eastern, Christianity.

Whether that made a difference in my life as a *natural born* American citizen is difficult for me to say, but many of the traits of working class German-American Lutherans—stubbornness, obstinacy, persistence, outspokenness, willfulness, and, yes, arrogance—have been used to describe me.

I was *shaped* by Western Christianity in the form of the Lutheran religion, and I grew up in the East End section of Pittsburgh, attended a Lutheran church where two of my uncles were deacons—and attended a parochial school through the eighth grade—with families named Schumann, Manka, Koehler, Sallach, Doege, Bucholz, Hatting, Kovak, and Benzenhoeffer.

All that had an impact.

As I recollect those days, close to seventy years ago, I remember that there were communion services in German offered to very old members of my parish church. My grandfather worked for a Pittsburgh brewery, and homemade beer and wine were a part of life, as were foods that surely would be banned from today's cholesterol-conscious tables.

Even on my father's side of the family—after years of Turkish oppression—there were residues of what at one time must have been a vibrant Christianity—fish on Friday, lamb at Easter, purple Easter eggs, and a prevalence of vegetarian dishes during Lent.

My life was unique in other ways also. My father was not employed—he was self-employed.

Upon returning from the Marine Corps in 1945, he used the GI Bill to open an oriental rug store. And there I grew up, the son of a merchant, living amidst what were considered luxury goods, but living above the store. Each day for eight years I walked two miles to East End Lutheran School, absolutely absorbed in the rituals of a Lutheran community unchanged for hundreds of years.

My year was governed by the ecclesiastical calendar with its seasons of the church year: Lent, Easter, Advent, and Christmas. During Lent, we attended Church services on Wednesday evenings, and Easter and Christmas were preceded by appropriate choral practice—all of us were in the school choir.

School days began with music, a homily, and prayer. Then we had classes until noon when we ate our bag lunches and played "bat ball" for half an hour in the church parking lot. More classes followed recess, and we ended the day with Vespers—more songs and prayer. My classmates and I experienced this for six years until, in seventh grade, we had confirmation classes tacked on.

Those were interesting classes, conducted by Pastor Frederick Schumann of First Trinity, who didn't leave much to chance. There was a great deal of memorization of Bible verses (I can still recite the books in the King James Bible) and entire passages from Luther's "Small Catechism" (many of which I can also still recite). I suspected that there was a "Large" catechism, but I didn't press the issue. This regimen would probably have been cruel punishment for many children ages six to thirteen, but for me it was the essence of life itself.

I enjoyed regular schoolwork, too, and did quite well—except for math. But the greater lesson I learned was the

existence of a spiritual and temporal order into which I was
expected to fit and that the greater claim on me was of a
spiritual order.

When my father reached forty years of age, he sold his
successful rug and carpet business in Pittsburgh and moved
to Miami, Florida, where I completed high school and saw
my parents' marriage end in divorce.

I loved Miami. And still do. The balmy weather, diversity
of population, entertainment, and tourist venues are attrac-
tive. I got to know them from a Lambretta motor scooter on
which I would take long rides. And my classmates and I
would visit a variety of places that others of our generation
would never see. Once, a classmate and I interviewed Jimmy
Hoffa at the Fontainebleau Hotel!

Though parochial school ended in grade eight, and even
though I found public junior high in Pittsburgh and high
school in Florida to be quite a change from the secure little
world I had enjoyed, I continued, as I had been taught, to
meditate on God's majestic creation—an order that met with
a responding chord in the depth of my soul and which
sustained me as I struggled to make my way in life. That, at
least, had not been challenged by the American public school
system.

Even though most of my public school teachers were
abysmal, the three exceptional teachers I encountered (speci-
fically, a French teacher in 9th grade, an English teacher in
12th grade, and my high school debate coach)—and extra-

curricular activities—made North Miami high school bearable.

I'm surprised that sixty years later I can remember the first and last name of one good teacher—Alan Stratton, a high school English teacher—and the last name of my debate coach, Mr. Handy.

Good literature and National Forensic League debating opened a new world for me, and I met my fellow "nerds"— Keith Barish, who later went into real estate, motion picture production [*Sophie's Choice* (1982), *The Running Man* (1987), and *The Fugitive* (1993)] and the restaurant business [Planet Hollywood], and Stanley Ringler, who became a rabbi and an executive with B'nai Brith in Washington.

I discovered that I was good at public speaking, but I was not as good as Neal Sonnet, a debater from Miami Beach High School, whose ability to give a speech was so great that you admired his ability even as you knew he was depriving you of a win. Neal became an assistant U. S. Attorney and Chief of the Criminal Division for the Southern District of Florida. In my experience, only Ronald Reagan came close to Neal's speaking ability.

From my Jewish friends in Miami, I came to appreciate how it felt to be a religious minority and learned about the State of Israel's struggle for survival. I did not need to learn about terrorism from books. Members of my Armenian family were early victims of Islamic terror.

As I noted earlier, my grandmother and her sisters escaped from Aleppo, Syria, to Cairo. One of her sisters stayed there. My grandmother came to the United States. There she married Hagop Bishirjian and gave birth to my father and his three siblings. Their generation faced the Great Depression and World War II, experiencing things that gave them traits, abilities, and character needed for life in post-World War II America. I remember family gatherings with marvelous foods that surely contributed to my love for cooking. So, while I may look like a German, I cook and eat like an Armenian.

Debating led to an interest in politics and my selection along with Stanley Ringler to attend Florida "Boys State" in Tallahassee. Florida was segregated in 1959, and Boys State was, too. I remember that Stanley and I earned the animosity of the delegates from northern Florida—fellows not unlike Bill Clinton, I suspect—when we motioned within the Boys State Senate that all future Florida Boys States be desegregated.

Our motion was defeated.

Our companion motion that no women be admitted was soundly defeated, also. In high school, I joined Junior Achievement, and my political and public speaking skills earned me a trip to the Junior Achievement national convention in the summer of 1960, where I made an unsuccessful run at the presidency of Junior Achievement.

When I entered the University of Pittsburgh as a freshman in 1960, my high school debate experience earned me a slot on the debate team of the William Pitt Debate Union, and my partner, Michael "Chick" Liebowitz, and I won several intercollegiate debates in our freshman and sophomore years, including tournaments at Annapolis and the University of London in Ontario, Canada.

In one of those sessions at the William Pitt Debate Union, I met Harry Woodruff Turner, "Mr. Republican," whose parents were Taft Republicans, and I joined the Young Republicans (YR). It was early fall, 1960, and the presidential election of that year captured our attention. Ed Flaherty, Chairman of the Allegheny County Republican Party, was the speaker at one of our YR meetings. Ed Flaherty was truly interested in young people and offered invitations to come and see him. I was bold enough to suggest that he give me a job.

He hired me on the spot.

That very week, after classes at Pitt, I started working the switchboard at Allegheny County Republican Party Headquarters and followed the course of Richard Nixon's ill-fated campaign for president against John F. Kennedy.

My experience included poll watching in Pittsburgh's Ward One, a thin strip of land that traverses Pittsburgh's "Point," passes the Civic Center, and terminates at what we called the "Hill District;" attending a campaign banquet with President Eisenhower, where I sat at the press table; attending a pep rally with Vice President Nixon; and serving as a bag man.

Well, almost a bag man.

One of the Republican County Headquarters staff asked me to accompany him to the outskirts of Pittsburgh where he stopped his car at the edge of an open field. He reached down under his seat and pulled out a bag which he gave to a man standing in the middle of the field. I had been the witness to a payoff thus sealing a political deal with a dissident labor union member.

I was eighteen years old.

Poll watching was also enlightening. I watched as voters in Ward 1, many of them vagrants, were given a marked paper ballot and told to deposit the marked ballot and return with an unmarked ballot. Whereupon the voter was paid ten dollars in cash, and the trunk of the car would open to reveal an array of whiskey bottles from which the voter would take a swig.

Just as my Republican leaders sinned, so were they sinned against by Pennsylvania Governor David Lawrence's Democrat Party machine, for whom the same ritual was standard, except the Democrats controlled the voting rolls and a surprising number of dead people voted for John F. Kennedy.

I don't recall any ill feelings.

The contest was governed by unwritten rules that *both* Republicans and Democrats followed in the understanding that next time, perhaps, we who lost might be the winners.

I sometimes contrast the practices of those days—more than sixty years ago—with the outrage expressed at Richard Nixon's Watergate caper, the strict Ethics in Government Legislation that was a result of that scandal, the Independent Counsel law, stricter campaign finance regulations, the common use of "walking-around money" to bribe community leaders, and the strictures that post-Watergate Democrats imposed on politics in America.

The United States had survived one hundred and eight years with no independent counsel, no ethics laws to speak of, massive infractions of campaign spending rules, and ritualized lying by the executive branch to the Congress and the American people.

Beginning with the presidency of John F. Kennedy in 1961, we deserted the Cubans we had recruited to invade Fidel Castro's Communist Cuba and watched while the Berlin Wall was constructed by the Soviet Union. We allowed fifty-eight thousand American boys to die in Vietnam, all without overt concern about ethics in government. After the American people had had enough and elected a Republican president, however, ethics in government became a prerequisite for holding political office.

As discussed in Chapter 10, this newfound righteousness that so permeates government, education, print, and elec-

tronic media today in reality is a cover for ideological partisanship by which the ruling class assures its hold on political power.

Should we be surprised by the mediocrity of so many
elected officials—Republican and Democrat—who grace our
newspapers and airwaves with statements lacking in intellectual depth or commitment to political principle? In such
a world, it is important to remember the great souls who
ennoble us.

Chapter 1

Henry Regnery, E. Victor Milione,
& Russell Kirk

Upon graduation from North Miami High School in 1960, I was admitted to the University of Pittsburgh. Though my father offered to pay my tuition at Florida State, I decided I would return to our former hometown, Pittsburgh, Pennsylvania, where I was admitted as an out-of-state student at the University of Pittsburgh. My grades were mediocre, and my SAT score was under what was required for admission to the Ivy League. I believe that had my father not moved our family to Miami, Florida, in 1958, it is unlikely that Pitt would have admitted me.

Instead of taking remedial courses at Pitt in Math, I avoided Math entirely and fulfilled my science requirements by taking courses in biology and geology. Because I had excelled in high school debates, however, I joined the William Pitt Debate Union. There I met Harry Woodruff Turner, known as "Woody," and joined him in founding the Society for Conservative Studies.

In 1961, I became an 18-year-old political conservative.

Early in the summer of 1960, a high school classmate and I drove nonstop from Miami to Chattanooga where he dropped me off. I took a Greyhound bus the remainder of the way to Pittsburgh. I pumped gas in my uncle's Gulf gas station and lived with my father's brother and his wife in an area of Regent Square on the fringe of Schenley Park.

There were three persons I met that year who were influential in launching me on my career: Ed Flaherty, who graciously gave me a part-time job; Harry Turner, who led me into the conservative movement; and James Malone, President of the Pennsylvania Manufacturers Association.

In January, 1961, after the 1960 Presidential election, "Woody" Turner came to a YR meeting with dozens of back issues of *National Review* and explained that we might have lost the 1960 election, but there was another campaign we could join. His parents were Taft Republicans, and meeting Woody was my introduction to the world of American conservatives.

The course of American history, and the Republican Party, would have been very different had Sen. Robert A. Taft (R-OH) won the GOP nomination for President in 1952. The liberal "Dewey" wing of the GOP, however, persuaded former General Dwight D. Eisenhower to seek the nomination. It took the conservative faction within the GOP another 28 years before a conservative won the Republican Party's presidential nomination in 1980.

The Ohio GOP never recovered, and today, though Ohio elects Republicans, they are at best "moderates" and at worst "Liberals." Sen. Taft died of pancreatic cancer in 1953, too soon to lead a conservative movement. There is nothing to remember him by except the Taft-Hartley "Right to Work" Act, officially known as the Labor-Management Relations Act passed by Congress on June 23, 1947, and a memorial Carillon located north of the U.S. Capitol on Constitution Avenue. I make it a point to drive by it whenever I'm in D.C.

None of that was known to me in 1961. Under Woody's direction, however, I became a debater in the William Pitt Debate Union and active in the Society for Conservative Studies. As a conservative activist on campus, I was supported by the Intercollegiate Studies Institute, which paid conservative speakers to visit campus conservative clubs, and by Sarah Mellon Scaife and James Malone.

Of the latter, Sarah Mellon Scaife and James Malone, President of the Pennsylvania Manufacturers Association (PMA), were the only adults in Pittsburgh who financially supported my activities. Miss Scaife donated a small sum to Pennsylvania Youth for Goldwater-Miller in 1964, and, beginning in 1962, I would periodically take a streetcar to downtown Pittsburgh and visit Mr. Malone in his PMA office on Grant Street. We would talk about Pittsburgh and national politics, and he would write a check in support of the Society.

The Pennsylvania Manufacturers Association financially supported the Republican Party leaders of the wards that divided the City of Pittsburgh and, at an annual Lincoln's Day banquet, brought everyone in the County Republican Party together for an evening of solidarity. I was invited to attend those dinners which fed my pride and my stomach.

As a result of that activism, my grades declined, but my spirits were strengthened by my search for understanding the condition of politics in my country. I felt we were on the wrong track. One of the congressmen I met at the Allegheny County headquarters, Rep. Bob Corbett, arranged for me to work as a GS-3 Clerk Typist at the General Services Administration (GSA) in Washington, D.C., and that summer, I lived with my mother's sister and interned at night at *Human Events.*

If America was careening toward socialism, I was in the best place for a political conservative to be—until the 1970s when I accepted a position as Assistant Professor of Government at the College of New Rochelle, a suburb of Westchester County, New York, made famous by George M. Cohan's musical of 1905 entitled *Forty-five Minutes from Broadway.* Irving Kristol had organized his friends in something known as "Neoconservatism," and I welcomed his friendship and the friendship of young people attracted to his immediate circle. But that stroke of good luck came eleven years after I'd interned at *Human Events.*

As an intern at *Human Events*, which Henry Regnery had a role in founding in 1944, I was present when the editors of the magazine, Frank Hanighen and James Wick, drew hundreds of conservatives from throughout the country to hold what they called a "Conservative Political Action Conference." I was able to attend, therefore, the first event that became CPAC.

Henry Regnery, founder of Regnery Publishing, was one of the vendors at these first conferences, and I was invited to manage his company's booth, so he could move about and make himself known to the many CPAC attendees. Several hundred conservatives from across the nation came to hear Sen. Strom Thurmond (D-SC) and other conservative politicians. One whom I spied was Sen. Harry Byrd (D-VA), pink-faced and wearing a white suit. Both Strom Thurmond and Harry Byrd were segregationists, and the District of Columbia, in 1960, controlled by Democrat Senators, was segregated, including street cars that had a white line in the middle of each car.

Unlike Senators Byrd and Thurmond, the conservatism of Henry Regnery was not racist, nor was that of Hanighen and Wick, and the three of them did much to shape a reputation of conservatism that was based on philosophical principles.

We know it today as "America First."

Those principles attracted Americans to read *Human Events* and *National Review* and the many books that Henry

Regnery published. One conservative who was an avid fan of *Human Events* and *National Review* was Ronald Reagan.

Henry Regnery was a very sophisticated student of European philosophy and resisted the socialism that suffused intellectual and political culture in the United States from World War I to the New Deal. He especially understood the damage done to American political culture by President Woodrow Wilson's decision to destroy balance-of-power politics by leading America's entry into World War I.

Like many political conservatives of that era and today, Henry Regnery was called an "isolationist." That term, of course, is a pejorative used by our ruling class who identify with the democratic project of Woodrow Wilson and who place improving the world ahead of the national interest.

I found Mr. Regnery to be very friendly, almost fatherly, and for my part, I enjoyed spending brief moments with him at two political action conferences in 1961 and 1962. One of the benefits of employment at those events was that I was allowed to take home any books that had been on display. Regnery Publishing was *the* premier publisher of philosophical conservatives. Here is a list of some of the many books that Henry Regnery published:

Hitler In Our Selves, Max Picard
Our Threatened Values, Victor Gollancz
The German Opposition to Hitler, Hans Rothfels

The Theory of Education in the United States, Albert Jay Nock

The High Cost of Vengeance, Freda Utley

Invasion 1944: Rommel and the Normandy Campaign, Lt.-Gen. Hans Speidel

Politics, Trials and Errors, Maurice Hankey

America's Second Crusade, William Henry Chamberlin

Eleven Years in Soviet Prison Camps, Elinor Lipper

The Techniques of Communism, Louis Budenz

The China Story, Freda Utley

4 Years in a Red Hell: Imprisonment in China, Very Rev. Harold W. Rigney, SVD

The Twenty-Year Revolution from Roosevelt to Eisenhower, Chesly Manly

Social Security: Fact and Fancy, Dillard Stokes

Check Off: Labor Bosses and Working Men, Jameson G. Campaigne

Many of these books that Henry Regnery published did not earn him plaudits, but two of the books that he published did more to shape a conservative "movement" in the United States than any others: Russell Kirk's *The Conservative Mind* and William F. Buckley's *God & Man at Yale*.

The conservative writer Lee Edwards writes in *A Brief History of the Modern American Conservative Movement*,[1] published in 2004, that four essential elements have made conservative ideas an effective force in American politics:

1. Conservative philosophers
2. Popularizers of conservative ideas
3. Philanthropists who support the ideas
4. Politicians who carry conservative ideas "in their hips"

The philosophers present their ideas in an academic forum. Their ideas, in turn, are popularized, and those ideas capture the minds of aspiring politicians. During this process, philanthropists support the writings of the philosophers and the journals in which their ideas are popularized, and they donate to the political campaigns of politicians.

Henry Regnery was #2 in what made us conservative.

From my internship at *Human Events* came two other persons I encountered who became friends and lifelong influences, namely E. Victor Milione and Russell Kirk.

That summer of 1961, the Intercollegiate Studies Institute (ISI) held a summer school for conservative students at C.W. Post College. Vic Milione, president of ISI, was there,

---

[1] Lee Edwards, *A Brief History of the American Conservative Movement* (Washington, D.C.: Heritage Foundation, 2004).

along with Russell Kirk, who led the week's discussions. Frank Chodorov and Lemuel Boulware also made appearances.

Chodorov founded ISI and recruited a young William F. Buckley, Jr., as its first president. Lem Boulware was the legendary head of General Electric's public education program who hired Hollywood actor Ronald Reagan to tour and speak at all GE manufacturing facilities.

Those ISI summer schools were instrumental in providing an education for students who were deprived of gaining a true education by the universities they attended. At an event I organized at which we conferred an Honorary MA in Government on E. Victor Milione, a former ISI summer school student, Judge Loren Smith, said that he attended as many ISI summer schools as he could and lamented that the colleges he attended were not as good.

I think it was Bill Schulz, then a writer for Fulton Lewis, who later became editor of *Reader's Digest*, who asked if I was going to ISI's summer school.

I jumped at the opportunity!

As interest in conservatism was growing among students, we sorted ourselves out into the scholarly and the activists. Young Americans for Freedom, a student group that Bill Buckley was instrumental in founding, attracted activists. Many were in a hurry to get into politics; some were in too much of a hurry. "The Sharon Statement,"[2] written by M. Stanton Evans, was the manifesto of Young Americans for Freedom, named after the Sharon, Connecticut, estate of Bill Buckley where the Statement was announced.

Among the attendees at this meeting were future and current conservative leaders, including Howard Phillips, historian Lee Edwards, Don Lipsett, Paul Niemeyer, Allan Ryskind, M. Stanton Evans, Bill Buckley of *National Review,* and his publisher William A. Rusher.

Though I appreciated YAF's role in growing our numbers, I had a feeling that we were pushed by some who wanted us on picket lines and not in our campus libraries. I had my hands full completing my course requirements at Pitt while engaging in campus conservative activities and had little time for picketing. Toward the end of that summer session, I shared my feelings with Vic Milione that we were being "used."

After that ISI summer school, and one other that I attended, I stayed in contact with ISI, and over a period of forty-six years, from 1973 to 2019, I published fourteen long essays in *Modern Age*, an ISI publication founded by Russell Kirk.

On December 6, 2007, Yorktown University gathered to honor Vic Milione with an honorary degree. Though we

---

[2] Available online at https://www.yaf.org/news/the-sharon-statement/

honored Vic Milione, some did not. He told me that when he told a potential donor that he was the head of ISI, that person said, "You're too short to lead a successful conservative organization." E. Victor Milione died on February 10, 2008. I attended his funeral and travelled in a caravan of several hundred automobiles to the cemetery where he was buried. T. Kenneth Cribb, Jr., later eulogized Milione at a memorial service on April 11, 2008, in Arlington, Virginia, in a way that helps characterize Milione's worldview:[3]

... Since his passing in February, I have been looking over the essays [Milione] published from time to time over the years, and I have been noting the authors he characteristically quoted. They can be grouped into a few categories that point to the heart of Vic's deepest concerns. First, there is the American experience—such writers as Tocqueville, Lord Bryce, and the authors of the Federalist Papers. Then there is the mission of a university—Cardinal Newman, Christopher Dawson, Jacques Barzun, and Mark van Doren. There is also the matter of faith and unbelief—Max Picard and C. S. Lewis preeminently. And finally there are writers addressing the crisis of the twentieth century—Sorokin, Ortega y

---

[3] T. Kenneth Cribb, Jr., "William F. Buckley Jr. and E. Victor Milione," ISI Archive (October 8, 2014). (Reprinted here with permission.) Available online at https://isi.org/intercollegiate-review/william-f-buckley-jr-and-e-victor-milione/

Gasset, and Richard Weaver, among others. Behind the
totalitarian threat of Soviet communism that loomed
over the century just past, behind the "revolution of
nihilism" that convulsed the world in the Second World
War, lay a deeper and more pervading problem in
modern times that could only be addressed at the level of
ideas. It was a problem of forgetting: of forgetting the
foundations of the achievement that is the West.

As he saw it, the central task of our time was therefore one of enculturation—a term he took from the
historian Christopher Dawson. Tocqueville had seen
that under the conditions of modernity, "every fresh
generation is a new people." In that fact lies the promise
of progress—but there is also a great and usually un-
recognized peril. The young have always been given to
hubris, failing to recognize the debts they owe and so
falling into ingratitude. But the progressive tendencies of
modern times fan this hubris to a white heat—and at
length, the ideologues proclaim that piety toward the
received inheritance of Western civilization is a superseded virtue, perhaps even a retrograde vice.

Here, then, was the central insight behind Vic's work.
If the great tradition of the West is to continue, there
must be a nurturing of the timeless principles that under-
gird our civilization among those who will be coming on
the scene. In the absence of continuity, "No generation
could link with another. Men would become little better

than [Burke's] flies of summer." Lacking a firm grounding in our heritage, the young would be prey to every fleeting enthusiasm and every totalitarian promise.

That was Vic. His wife Amalia, affectionately known as "Mali," was a perfect companion. Of the two photos I cherish of me and Vic Milione, one includes Barry Goldwater; Mali and Vic; and ISI regional directors, Bob Luckock and Fred Andre. The second was taken when Yorktown University conferred on Vic Milione the honorary MA in Government.

From left: Barry Goldwater, Mali, Vic, Bob Luckock, Fred Andre, & me

When I first met Vic, the offices of ISI were in an office building in downtown Philadelphia. The building had a club on an upper floor, and after we finished our meeting, Vic would invite us to have a drink. He told me once that he sent a copy of a book entitled *Income Tax: The Root of All Evil* by Frank Chodorov to the IRS. I asked why he did that since the IRS is not known for its humor. He laughed and said, "I don't know."

From left: Vic Milione & me

Russell Kirk gave lectures every morning during that week at C.W. Post College, and after dinner some nights, he would tell ghost stories. Even today, I get a shiver when I think of a person looking in on Russell through a window of his family home in Mecosta, Michigan. This photo of Russell by Jay McNally captures his spirit.

That week of "summer school" with Russell Kirk was too long ago, so I do not remember much that he taught, but I remember his appreciation for the Irish statesman, Edmund

Burke. In one semester, during my years at the University of
Pittsburgh, I took a directed reading course on Edmund
Burke from a Pitt English professor and purchased a set of
The Works of The Right Honorable Edmund Burke.[4]

Russell Kirk

I was much taken with Russell Kirk's love for Burke and
intrigued by his study of John Randolph of Roanoke. The
first essay I published appeared in Pitt's undergraduate literary magazine, *Ideas and Figures*, in 1964 and was entitled *A
Vocabulary of Conservatism*. I sent a copy of that essay, along
with my application for admission, to the University of
Notre Dame's graduate Department of Government's chairman, Fr. Stanley Parry, CSC.

---

[4] *The Works of The Right Honorable Edmund Burke*, 8th
edition (Boston: Little, Brown, 1884).

My education at Notre Dame with Fr. Stanley Parry, Gerhart Niemeyer, and Eric Voegelin diminished my admiration for Edmund Burke, but not for Russell Kirk. *The Conservative Mind* was my introduction to a body of literature, politics, and philosophy that supported the truths of my Lutheran upbringing, namely respect for authority, preference for ideas over action, the philosophy of limited government enshrined in the Constitution of the United States, and love of God and my country.

A seminar with Russell Kirk, unlike a seminar with any instructor at Harvard, was an opportunity to learn the truths that we shared with the generation of Americans who gave our nation its foundation in law, faith, and patriotism. Matthew Continetti writes in *The Forgotten Father of American Conservatism* that Kirk's "literary output of more than 20 books of nonfiction, three novels, hundreds of articles and book reviews, and some 3,000 syndicated columns" was remarkable.[5]

At some point, perhaps in 1982, I offered to retain the Southern writers, William and Joyce Corrington, to write a script for a low-budget film based on Russell Kirk's *The Roots of American Order*. Since Russell had sold the rights to

---

[5] Matthew Continetti, "The Forgotten Father of American Conservatism," *The Atlantic* (October 19, 2018). Available online at https://www.theatlantic.com/ideas/archive/2018/10/russell-kirk-father-american-conservatism/573433/

that book to Pepperdine University, Russell and I were invited to Pepperdine to discuss the purchase of the rights to base the film on that book. Upon our arrival, a luncheon banquet was held in Russell's honor. I still remember that grapes served at this luncheon were coated with a crust of crystalline sugar.

Pepperdine is a Church of Christ institution, and Russell Kirk was revered by the administration at Pepperdine. When I got around to negotiating with Pepperdine's counsel, however, the gloves were off, and I was offered an agreement that benefited Pepperdine rather than the scholar just honored at lunch. Pepperdine University, like every other university, is a "taker" not a "giver."

I acceded to the terms of the agreement because I felt the venture was worth the effort. Bill Corrington and his wife agreed to the fee I offered them, and a television producer was chosen with whom the Corringtons had previously worked. A tour of locations in Europe was conducted, and the Corringtons settled in to writing a film script.

I had served as Chairman of the National Endowment for the Humanities (NEH) on the "Transition Team" in the Office of the President-Elect in 1980, and I made application for an NEH grant to produce a film based on Russell Kirk's *The Roots of American Order*. William Bennett had been confirmed as chairman of NEH. A registered Democrat, Bennett was known for *The Book of Virtues* and a gambling addiction, and it was assumed by some that he was a political conservative. In fact, Bennett is a neoconservative, and he assigned a neoconservative program manager to review our NEH application. Our proposal was rejected.

The reason: the Constitution is Lockean, not Burkean.

I am not a spiteful person, but when Bennett's gambling became front page news, I sent him this letter on stationery of Yorktown University:

May 6, 2003

Dear Bill:

By this time, everyone has an opinion—and told you.

I was in New York on Saturday to attend an event at the Waldorf, but I left my hotel at 59th Street and walked to 9th and 54th to purchase a Racing Form, go to Ned Kelly's bar, and blow about $60 on losers in the Derby.

I am a professional handicapper, or, I should say, I like odds that I can control.

That involves lots of research, experience and hunches. I'm always looking for a horse that slobbers and can't walk straight. That's a winner, because the owner has administered a "milk shake," a concoction of bicarbonate that causes horses to run like hell.

My bets are modest, however, and probably counter-productive for that reason. But the intellectual challenge that each race offers keeps me young at a time when Internet companies are making people into old wrecks.

So, my friend, keep your head up, forgive your enemies, and look for a horse that slobbers. Since you don't bet any more, call me when you see one.

With very best wishes,

Sincerely yours,

Richard J. Bishirjian, Ph.D.
President

Despite its low budget and a great deal of effort, after the rebuke by NEH, I could not raise the funding to produce the film. Russell Kirk was quite gracious in defeat, though in retrospect we both might have done some injury to Bill Bennett's ambition to become U.S. Secretary of Education.

In 2010, consistent with my admiration for Russell Kirk, I developed a distance learning, Internet-based course on *The Roots of American Order* with Colorado University's Classics professor, E. Christian Kopff and Northwood Institute's Glenn Moots. Here's the syllabus for that course:

COURSE SYLLABUS

1. **Course Number/Title:** Govt200, Russell Kirk's *Roots of American Order*, Part One. From Ancient Israel to the rise of Christianity.

Credit: Non-credit

Faculty: Richard J. Bishirjian, Ph.D., Glenn Moots, and
Christian Kopff, Ph.D.

2. **Course Description:** Govt200, *Roots of American Order,
   Part One,* is based on Russell Kirk's book of the same
   name to introduce students to American political
   thought. Kirk's work interprets the origins of the
   American nation and its constitutional order through an
   examination of the intellectual sources that shaped the
   American Founding. Part Two of *Roots of American
   Order* covers the period from the Puritan Revolution in
   England to the Philadelphia Convention.

   Russell Kirk employs the term "American Founding" broadly. Rather than fixing the American Founding
   at the date in 1776 of America's declaration of its independence from British rule, Kirk focuses on the
   origins of a whole complex of constitutions and laws,
   political bodies, traditions, mores, and habits that
   supported the emergence of the American people and
   nation. Thus, in Kirk's assessment, the emergence of a
   new American nation and government reveals the country's participation in the history of the West and did not
   reflect a radical break from the past. There were many
   influences that shaped the American Founding, not
   merely the Enlightenment concepts of John Locke. The

American Founding represents an attempt to defend an existing political culture that had deep historical roots. Kirk argues that our political institutions cannot be understood properly—or even function properly—if American citizens lose their connection with the living roots of their political order. A process of deculturation of this patrimony is the greatest threat today to American freedom.

3. **Course Goals:** After completing this course, students will recognize the imperative to reflect deeply about and make the case for the connections in the American experience between past and present and between moral and political order as the basis for civic virtue and public service. Students will leave the course with an ability to discuss the moral, institutional, and political significance of the arguments of the American Founding to contemporary American life.

4. **Course Learning Outcomes:** At the conclusion of the course, students will be able to

   a) Describe the multiple ways in which religion (Judaic and Christian) has influenced American political life.
   b) Compare and contrast the various classical regimes and recognize classical influences on the making of the American Republic.

c) Compare and contrast the concept of "virtue" in its classical, Christian, and modern meanings and apply it to American thinking about the moral foundations of society.

d) Describe the causes of the fall of the Roman Empire and the Christian response to the collapse of traditional order.

e) List the main contributions of English Protestantism to the formation of American colonial order.

5. Course Concepts

a) Influence of Judeo-Christian tradition on American colonists;

b) Influence of classical (ancient Greek and Roman) philosophy, history, and virtues on American thinking regarding the best regime;

c) Ancient concepts of virtue contrasted to the emergence of the virtue of Christian righteousness;

d) The problem of the radical imperfection of earthly justice in light of the city of God;

e) The English Bill of Rights

6. Required Texts

Kirk, Russell. *The Roots of American Order*. 4th ed. Wilmington, DE: ISI Books, 2003.

ISBN13: 978-1882926992. Purchase online at
https://isi.org/books/the-roots-of-american-order/
$14.40. Kindle: $11.99

King James Version of the Bible.
http://www.kingjamesbibleonline.org

7. **How this Course Works:** Govt200 is offered on a not-for-credit basis without instructor engagement. Students may take a ten-question multiple-choice quiz at the end of each session and a comprehensive final quiz. Multiple choice quizzes are automatically graded.

8. **Rent a Professor Option:** Students who desire engagement with a qualified instructor may choose our "Rent a Professor" option. Your instructor will evaluate your assignments and upon successful completion of coursework you will be awarded a badge.

9. **How You Will Be Graded:** Students who Rent a Professor will complete four assignments for assessment by their professor.

   a. **Weekly Quizzes.** At the end of every session, there is a ten-question multiple-choice quiz. Each quiz has four possible answers. Students may take weekly quizzes two times. Each quiz is graded automatically.

Weekly quizzes will be valued at 15% of the final grade. (15%)

b. **Final Comprehensive Quiz.** A final multiple-choice quiz will give students an opportunity to evaluate how well they've mastered all course content. Each question has four possible answers. There are thirty questions in the final quiz. The final quiz is valued at 15% of the final grade. (15%)

c. **Web-based Research Exercises** (30%). A Web-based research assignment is in Sessions 1, 2, 3, 4 and 5.

d. **Book Review (40%).** Students who are earning a badge through our Rent a Professor option are asked to write a five-page book review of any one of the following eight books.

- Russell Kirk, *The Conservative Mind: From Burke to Eliot,* 7th ed. (Gateway Editions, 2001). ASIN: B002CJM6CC. Kindle: $9.99.
- Plutarch, *Lives* (Digireads Publishing, 2018). ASIN: B07C89LVMS. Kindle: $7.49.
- Anthony Everett, *The Rise of Rome: The Making of the World's Greatest Empire.* ASIN: B0067AMRD0 Kindle: $9.99

- David Hackett Fisher, *Albion's Seed: Four British Folkways in America* (Oxford University Press, 1991). ASIN: B000SEKM9C. Kindle: $14.39.
- Glenn Moots, *Politics Reformed: The Anglo-American Legacy of Covenant Theology* (University of MO, 2010). ASIN: B004JXXKY2. Kindle, $42.70.
- Bruno Snell, *The Discovery of the Mind: The Greek Origins of European Thought* (Dover Publications, 2011, 1982, 1953). ASIN: 0486242641. Kindle: $9.99.
- Christian Kopff, *The Devil Knows Latin: Why America Needs the Classical Tradition* (Intercollegiate Studies Institute, 2014). ASIN: B00KFTZN58. Kindle: $14.99.
- Thomas M. Lindsay, *A History of the Reformation* (Library of Alexandria 2012). ASIN: B094D1BRFR. Kindle, $1.98.

10. **Students who choose to "Rent a Professor"** will also earn a richly coded badge for successful completion of coursework. All badges may be posted on Facebook.

Three badges may be earned for successful course completion:

Gold 92-100 to 90-91; (A) 4.00 (A-) 3.67
Silver 88-89 to 82-87; (B+) 3.30 (B) 3.00
Bronze 80-81 to 78-79; (B-) 2.67 (C+) 2.3

11. **Optional Discussion Topics**: Optional Topics for Discussion are posted in sessions one through five. Students are encouraged to create a discussion group and invite fellow students to join them in discussing these topics. Students not desiring to participate in a discussion group may still find that a review of posted comments will yield interesting information and insights into course content for each session. We recommend two public discussion forums.

   a) Google Groups.

   b) Yahoo Message Boards.

12. Summary of Assessments for Students Earning Badges:

   Weekly Quizzes (15%)
   Book Review (40%)
   Web-based Research Exercise (30%)
   Comprehensive Quiz (15%)

COURSE SCHEDULE

Recommended for course completion.

Session 1: The Hebrew World – Revelation

Introduction to Russell Kirk's concept of "order" as he intends it in the book's title. The first root of American order, Kirk says, derives from the ancient Hebrews.

Required Reading:

Kirk, *Roots*, "Order: The First Need of All," Chapter. 1, pp. 3-10.
Kirk, *Roots*, "The Law and the Prophets," Chapter 2, pp. 10-49.
Kopff, "Commentary on *Roots*, Chapter 2"
http://www.kingjamesbibleonline.org/
Genesis 12:1-7
Exodus 3:1-20
Exodus 20:1-20
Exodus 24:1-18
Jeremiah 2:1-37
Ezekiel 3:16-19
Ezekiel 11:16-21
Ezekiel 18:21-32

Web Research Exercise Topics: Surf the web for five sources on ancient Israel, summarize their content, and upload that document.

Optional Discussion Topics: Choose a topic. Submit a response and wait for responses by other students. Comment on their responses and choose a second topic.

1. Russell Kirk writes that "an order is bigger than its laws." What is the order revealed by the Hebrew experience? Is it relevant to American laws?

2. God's presence (indicated in the name "Yahweh") was revealed to the Hebrews, Kirk suggests, as the source of their personal and political order. Is a direct connection to God required for right political order in a non-theocratic society such as ours?

3. Russell Kirk asserts that "all the aspects of any civilization arise out of a people's religion: its politics, its economics, its arts, its sciences, even its simple crafts are the byproducts of religious insights and a religious cult." Describe what you think Kirk means by that statement. Then describe how it applies to contemporary America.

4. Russell Kirk writes that "an order is bigger than its
    laws." What is the difference between the order of
    laws and order itself? How is order itself "bigger"?

Session 2: The Greek World – Philosophy

This session presents the classical heritage that informed
American thinking about the best regime, its lawmakers
and statesmen, and how the Founders intended to avoid
the typical causes of a decent regime's decay.

Required Reading:

- Kirk, *Roots*, "Glory and Ruin: The Greek World,"
  Ch. 3, pp. 51-95.
- Bishirjian, "Commentary on *Roots*, Ch. 3" Summary of the Legislation of Solon
- http://www.agathe.gr/democracy/solon_the_law
  giver.html – Plato's *Republic* (Selections)
- http://www.perseus.tufts.edu/hopper/text?doc=
  Perseus:text:1999.01.0168 – Aristotle's *Politics*
  (Selections)
- http://www.online-literature.com/aristotle/politics/

Recommended Reading:

Dr. Kirk comments at length about the Athenian statesman, Solon. The principal source for Solon is Plutarch. There are several translations of Plutarch's life of Solon.

- "Solon," from Plutarch's *Lives* http://www.bostonleadershipbuilders.com/plutarch/solon.htm
- http://penelope.uchicago.edu/Thayer/E/Roman/Texts/Plutarch/Lives/Solon*.html
- http://www.perseus.tufts.edu/hopper/text?doc=Plut.%20Sol.

Web Research Exercise Topics: Surf the web for five sources on the history of ancient Greece, summarize their content, and upload that document.

Optional Discussion Topics: Choose a topic. Submit a response and wait for responses by other students. Comment on their responses and choose a second topic.

1. Socrates says in Plato's *Republic* that the Cave Image is a parable of human nature in its ignorance and

education. What conclusions do you draw about human nature and the nature of education?

2. Is Socrates suggesting that a spiritual education is the key to the right order of society?

3. Aristotle is concerned with these questions: "Who should rule?" and "What is the best constitution?" How would you evaluate the order of the American regime if you applied Aristotle's criterion of a good regime (one that serves the common good)?

4. In Book Three of the *Politics*, Aristotle lists the types of constitutions. Which one best describes the American regime?

5. What was it about Solon that appealed to the Founding generation?

Session 3: The Roman World—Republic and Empire

Despite the signal importance of the Greeks in posing the fundamental questions and formulating key concepts and theories of political philosophy, the Romans were closest to the hearts of American statesmen because of their stance on civic virtue. This session considers that affinity.

Required Reading:

- Kirk, *Roots*, "Virtue and Power: The Roman Tension," Ch. 4, pp. 97-136.
- Kopff, "Commentary on *Roots*, Ch. 4"
- Cicero's *On Duties*, Book III http://www.bostonleadershipbuilders.com/cicero/duties/book3.htm

Recommended Reading:

- Marcus Tullius Cicero from Plutarch's *Lives* http://www.bostonleadershipbuilders.com/plutarch/cicero.htm

Web Research Exercise Topics: Surf the web for five sources on ancient Rome, summarize their content, and upload that document.

Optional Discussion Topics: Choose a topic. Submit a response and wait for responses by other students. Comment on their responses and choose a second topic.

1. Most educated Americans of the revolutionary era were keenly interested in the history of Rome and intrigued by Rome's rise and fall. Why do you think the Roman experience in particular was so important to them? Are there lessons from Roman history applicable to the United States today?

2. Russell Kirk suggests that the "higher law tradition" of American jurisprudence can be traced to Cicero's idea of natural law and America's republican virtues, ideas most poignantly expressed by Virgil. Yet there is little talk today by American leaders of natural law or republican virtue. Why do you think that is the case, and is this something to be concerned about?

3. How does Russell Kirk describe the place of natural law in the context of Roman political thought and practice? Does the Roman approach apply to today's treatment of natural law in terms of, say, human rights?

4. Discuss Russell Kirk's observation that the "higher law tradition" of American jurisprudence can be traced to Cicero's idea of natural law and America's republican virtues can be traced to the Roman poet Virgil.

5. How does the "law of nature" referred to by American patriots differ from the "natural law" as referred to by Cicero and explained by Russell Kirk, and what are the consequences of that difference?

Session 4: The Rise of Christianity, the Fall of Rome

This session considers how the introduction of Christianity into the West developed or transformed classical ideas of "virtue" and "order."

Required Reading:

- Kirk, *Roots*, "The Genius of Christianity," Ch. 5, pp. 137-175.
- Bishirjian, "Commentary on *Roots*, Ch. 5"
- St. Augustine's *City of God*
- Book XIV, Chapter 28, and Book XIX
  http://www.newadvent.org/fathers/120114.htm and
  https://www.newadvent.org/fathers/120119.htm

Web Research Exercise Topics: Surf the web for five sources on St. Augustine, summarize their content, and upload that document.

Optional Discussion Topics: Choose a topic. Submit a response and wait for responses by other students. Comment on their responses and choose a second topic.

1. How does Augustine understand the spiritual virtues and the spiritual foundations of society? Does his analysis improve on that of the Greeks?

2. Russell Kirk argues that St. Augustine is a "Christian realist." What is the nature of Augustine's realism? Is St. Augustine too pessimistic about what can be done politically?

3. Based on your reading of *Roots*, Chapter 5, what explains the success of Christianity?

4. Is St. Augustine's division of mankind into two cities relevant today?

Session 5: The Reformation

This session explores the American intellectual heritage of the Reformation in England and English Protestant ideas.

Required Reading:

- Kirk, *Roots*, "The Reformers' Drum," Chapter 7, pp. 229-258.
- Moots, "Commentary on *Roots*, Ch. 7"

Web Research Exercise Topics: Surf the web for five sources on the Reformation, summarize their content, and upload that document.

Optional Discussion Topics: Choose a topic. Submit a response and wait for your instructor's response. Comment on that response and choose a second topic.

1. Russell Kirk writes of the "the Protestant character" of American attitudes about society. Does this Protestant character continue to exert a major influence in America today?

2. Colonial Americans were proud of their English heritage of liberty and celebrated historical efforts in England to check the powers of both church and state. Yet American appropriation of English precedents was selective, and proponents of American "exceptionalism" might emphasize how America

departed from old English ways. How much does the American Republic owe to the English?

3.   Interpret the English Bill of Rights (1689) in light of Kirk's summary of English history during this period.

4.   What lessons did American colonials draw from the violent struggles between Parliamentary forces and the King during the English Civil War?

5.   What is the Protestant ethic?

Chapter 2

William F. Buckley & Frank Meyer

I consider myself fortunate for having entered the University of Pittsburgh when I did. Six years earlier in 1954, Russell Kirk had published *The Conservative Mind.* Five years earlier in 1955, William F. Buckley, Jr., had started *National Review.* I encountered my William Pitt Debate Union leader, Harry "Woody" Turner. Woody was a Pitt senior and knowledgeable about political conservatism. One of the first things he did, after organizing the Society for Conservative Studies, was invite Bill Buckley to speak on campus.

That was 1961.

Again, that was too long ago for me to remember anything but Buckley's accent. It wasn't British English, but it sounded like what we called "highfalutin'"—enunciated with high and low intonations and marked by raised eyebrows. Buckley, compared to my friends and neighbors from Pittsburgh, was exotic. After his lecture, we crossed the street and took lunch at an expensive restaurant—where Buckley not only ordered wine but also picked up the tab. I will never forget that French Pomerol, as blissfully light red in color as

a watermelon and well-suited to our intellectual disposi-
tions. Pomerol is a wine regarded for its *quality* in Roman
times.

Avid reading of *National Review* improved my vocabulary, but not perfectly. In 1963, I arranged for Bill Buckley
to give another lecture at Pitt and drove to Pittsburgh's
airport to pick him up in my 1951 Dodge. The ride from the
airport takes travelers though a tunnel, and suddenly,
Pittsburgh's impressive skyline is revealed. Buckley was
astonished by the grandeur of that view, and I felt proud of
my city.

At the lecture, I introduced Buckley as editor of *National
Review,* which I described as the "conscience of America."
The large audience responded by hoots and the sound of feet
stomping on the floor. It was a set-up. Liberal friends came
to the lecture intending to jeer. As we walked back to my car,
Buckley said he had never experienced a response to such
hyperbole. Later that day, I looked up the word "hyperbole"
in a dictionary.

I read many of the books authored by *National Review*
correspondents or cited in the pages of *National Review.*
James Burnham's *The Managerial Revolution,* Frank
Meyer's *In Defense of Freedom,* Russell Kirk's *The Conservative Mind* and Hayek's *The Road to Serfdom* are four that
come to mind. One that made the greatest impact was cited
several times, and I purchased Eric Voegelin's *The New
Science of Politics.* Before that book arrived, I had read with

interest essays by Fr. Stanley Parry, CSC, a Catholic priest who was chairman of the Department of Government at the University of Notre Dame and made out an application for admission to Notre Dame's graduate school.

If I had never read *National Review*, my life would have been radically different.[1]

Two other persons I invited to speak, in addition to Bill Buckley, were William Rusher and Frank Meyer. Bill Rusher was publisher of *National Review* and known for his meticulous attire and orderly office. I was impressed by a simile he used to describe Liberalism. "Like a diamond prepared for cutting into a precious jewel, Liberalism cannot be destroyed, only broken into parts."

A former colleague who had worked at *National Review* told me that one day *National Review*'s staff decided to tease him and rearranged the names on his filing cabinets. He immediately noticed the changes and told them, "Put things back by the time I return," and left the office. Frank Meyer was a more friendly personality. When I met him, he had formulated a theory of "Fusionism," a way to weaponize conservatism as a marketable ideology.

Fusing the philosophic principles of Western order with Libertarian ideology was an attempt that Mario Pei, who was then a visiting scholar-in-residence at Pitt, told me was

---

[1] Richard Bishirjian, "The Creation of a Conservative Intellectual: 1960-65," in *Modern Age* (Winter, 1998).

"solipsistic." Solipsism is based on the projection of oneself as the source of reality, as if we ourselves are prior to and "make" reality.

Frank Meyer was certainly given to ideological constructions and joined the Communist Party as a result. Once he saw the error of his ways, however, he left the Party but was paranoiac in the belief that he was a target for assassination. He reversed his style of life by sleeping during the day and remaining awake during the night. His wife and two sons were subjected to this inverse style of life, and after Frank's death, his wife Elsie committed suicide.

Despite his unconventional life history, the Frank Meyer I met was likable. When he talked, he drew you into his confidence, and I appreciated that since I was a pariah at Pitt for advocating a conservative political philosophy and working on the 1964 Goldwater campaign for President.

Chapter 3

F. Clifton White and Sen. Barry Goldwater (R-AZ)

Twelve years after Bob Taft's defeat at the GOP convention, conservatives struggled to retake the presidency that had fallen to John F. Kennedy in 1960. Arizona Senator Barry Goldwater and JFK agreed to debate one another in 1964 if Goldwater were the Republican nominee. Tragically, President Kennedy was assassinated by a Communist sympathizer in Dallas in November, 1963. Goldwater wisely understood that JFK's Vice-President and successor, Lyndon Johnson, would be elected in his own right in 1964 and parked his ambition to run for President.

Barry Goldwater was heir to the Goldwater Department Store fortune in Arizona. His hobbies were photography and ham radio and a leave-us-alone attitude toward the federal government. The Right to Life movement had not yet arisen, and like many wives of Republican officeholders at the time, Goldwater's wife, Peggy, supported Planned Parenthood. Goldwater's taciturn political views later in his Senate career led him to lose the support of the conservative faithful, and his second wife, a political liberal, took offense at the conservative political stance of Arizona's Goldwater Institute.

Goldwater, essentially, was a small-time local politician and organized his political career around a small group of Arizonans whom he trusted, including Denison Kitchel and Dean Burch. With little appreciation for persons he did not know personally, coupled with a deficient college education, Goldwater lacked the character needed to reach out to national conservative leaders. While Bill Buckley shaped the conservative movement from his journal, and Russell Kirk led an intellectual revival in the principles of the culture of the West, Barry Goldwater simply symbolized an anti-big government attitude sharpened by his personal disdain for President Lyndon Johnson.

But he was a member of the United States Senate and an avowed conservative. The Senator was persuaded to approve Bill Buckley's brother-in-law, Brent Bozell, to ghost-write a political testament of what the Senator believed was his political philosophy.

Conscience of a Conservative, published in 1960, revolutionized the standing of Senator Goldwater and gave the conservative movement one book that articulated a political philosophy of a growing political movement.

So popular has *Conscience of a Conservative* become that political commentator Paul Krugman, political activists Wayne Root and Gary Chartier, and politicians Zell Miller and Jeff Flake have published books with variations on that title.[1]

Richard Mellon Scaife had become active as a political conservative and had hired a communications professional at U.S. Steel, R. Daniel McMichael, to manage his political interests. Dan McMichael and F. Clifton White were friends, and McMichael encouraged White's efforts to promote the candidacy of Barry Goldwater for president. I became acquainted with Dan McMichael and got to know Cliff White. The efforts of White's "Draft Goldwater Committee" were not well tied to the Senator's ambitions and, especially after the assassination of President Kennedy, Goldwater had no interest in running in 1964. But the clamor for a champion to lead the faithful into the promised land reached hysterical levels.

Why Goldwater decided to run, when he knew he would lose, was due solely to his patriotism. At the very least, by accepting the GOP nomination for president, Goldwater

---

[1] Paul Krugman, *The Conscience of a Liberal* (2007), Zell Miller, *A National Party No More: The Conscience of a Conservative Democrat* (2003), Wayne Allyn Root, *The Conscience of a Libertarian: Empowering the Citizen Revolution with God, Guns, Gold & Tax Cuts* (2009), Gary Chartier, *The Conscience of an Anarchist: Why It's Time to Say Good-Bye to the State and Build a Free Society* (2011), Jeff Flake, *Conscience of a Conservative: A Rejection of Destructive Politics and a Return to Principle* (2017).

could express his disdain for big government, his belief that LBJ was engaged in a war in Vietnam with no commitment to victory and, had he not run, the nomination would have fallen to Liberal Internationalist, Nelson Rockefeller. The outcome was disastrous with losses of GOP members in the U.S. House of Representatives exceeded only by the number of losses in 2018.

I attended the first Draft Goldwater rally in Madison Square Gardens organized by Cliff White in 1962 and was appointed Youth for Goldwater chairman for Pennsylvania. But, Barry Goldwater, like Ronald Reagan, represented the World War II generation that had no interest in developing younger successors. The youth campaign was a top-down affair run from Washington by a budding political operative, James Harff, and support for the "Youth for Goldwater" volunteers in the States consisted of dropping down when convenient to hold large rallies. Thanks to Dick Scaife, one rally was held on the lawn of the University of Pittsburgh, but the national campaign gave us no other support.

Jim Harff later became a D.C. lobbyist but was largely unknown to the tens of thousands of young people attracted to his part of the Goldwater campaign. F. Clifton "Cliff" White was rejected for the chairmanship of the Republican National Committee. Goldwater's buddy, Dean Burch, took that role, and White, nearly bankrupt, found work in Venezuela where he used American campaign techniques to win the election of a socialist, Carlos Andres Perez, head of the Democratic Action Party. Once elected, President Perez gave diplomatic recognition to the government of Cuba, facilitated transfer of the Panama Canal to Panama, nationalized the iron and petroleum industries, and invested in large state-owned industrial projects for the production of aluminum and hydroelectric energy and for the funding of social welfare and scholarship programs that involved massive government spending. The problems of Venezuela today can be traced to Cliff White.

Ever since November, 1964, the phrase "Goldwater Cycle" portrayed the dilemma of the GOP as it faced presidential elections.[2] According to the Goldwater Cycle theory, if the GOP nominates a true believer, the party will go down to defeat. Donald Trump's election in 2016 proved that theory wrong.

While in college, I worked on both the 1960 Nixon and the 1964 Goldwater campaigns and have some personal understanding of the way it was back then.

In 1963, campaign manager Cliff White ramped up a campaign, begun in 1961, to draft Arizona Senator Barry Goldwater for President. On November 22 of that year, President John F. Kennedy was assassinated. The outpouring of emotion that was the result of that crime covered over

---

[2] Richard Bishirjian, "A Goldwater Cycle?" *Chronicles* (April 7, 2015). Available online at
https://www.chroniclesmagazine.org/article/a-goldwater-cycle/

the weaknesses of JFK as he entered the 1964 campaign for re-election. We will never know if a reprise of the Nixon campaign, or even a Goldwater candidacy, would have been successful if JFK had lived, but we do know what did happen.

Lyndon B. Johnson succeeded to the Presidency and committed himself to a continuation of the Kennedy legacy and then, upon being elected in his own right, jumped his administration into overdrive. Sen. Barry Goldwater knew that LBJ was not just a crook but that he was also a New Deal Democrat who would revive the attack on limited govern-ment begun by FDR in 1933. Against his better judgment that he couldn't win, Goldwater sought the GOP nomination and went down to colossal defeat in November, 1964.

The GOP lost thirty-six House seats, giving Johnson a two-thirds majority in the House, and the two seats gained in the U.S. Senate gave Johnson a two-thirds majority in the Senate. That control of Congress in 1965, not unlike the control of Congress won in 2016, enabled LBJ to enact a bevy of Great Society programs and to escalate a ground war in Asia—something he denied he would do during the 1964 campaign. As a result of what LBJ called "that bitch, Vietnam," more than 50,000 Americans lost their lives, and war weariness assured the election of Richard Nixon in 1968.

There was no assassinated President in 2016, and the Democrats nominated a woman, but the GOP had been controlled by centrists since the mantle of Ronald Reagan was passed to George H. W. Bush. The Republican Party's grassroots activists, energized by a conservative rebellion of Tea Party activists, were straining to move the GOP away from the moderate faction that controlled it.

The cumulative impact of eight years of George "W" Bush as "decider," however, had created a weariness with imperial wars in the American public that drove the candidacy of Barack Obama and also drove the appeal of Rand Paul and Donald Trump.

The United States' entry into World War I was intended by President Wilson to destroy "balance of power" politics and replace it with democratic idealism. George "W" Bush did not articulate his democratic idealism when he committed American troops in 2003 to an invasion of Iraq, but, by 2005, "W" was confident that, in his Second Inaugural, he could reveal his desire to return to a form of idealism associated with Woodrow Wilson.

I argue in *The Conservative Rebellion* that by hiring speechwriter Michael Gerson, "W" signaled, before he ran for the GOP nomination in 2000, that he was motivated by the religious ideas that would control the foreign policies of his Administration.

"The best hope for peace in our world," the President said in his Second Inaugural, "is the expansion of democracy in all the world," with the ultimate goal "of ending tyranny in our world." That extreme idea led to decisions by the "decider" that destroyed the balance of power in the

Middle East. A collateral casualty was the GOP limited government brand.

Rand Paul and Donald Trump signaled opposition to "imperial" foreign policies of the United States by emphasizing that only Congress has the power to declare war. Rand Paul opposed the excesses of the Patriot Act and the killing of American citizens suspected of terrorist ties without due process of law.

The campaign of Ted Cruz, like that of Bobby Jindal, Rick Santorum, Marco Rubio, John Kasich, and Scott Walker, however, emphasized the opposite—active use of military power to destroy ISIS and support Israel, if necessary, in military action to destroy Iran's nuclear weapons program. Their rhetorical appeal to "American exceptionalism" signaled their sympathy with "W"'s revival of Woodrow Wilson's democratic idealism and his advocacy of war to make the world democratic.

If there is such a thing as a Goldwater cycle, it could only be reprised by a true outsider who, like Barry Goldwater, would advocate a realist policy in foreign affairs and limited, Constitution-based, domestic policies.

That excluded Scott Walker, Bobby Jindal, Jeb Bush, John Kasich, Rick Santorum, and Marco Rubio who appear to have fallen into a "time warp" aligned with George "W" Bush who broke the GOP limited government brand and revived Wilsonian idealism.

Donald Trump understood that if he rallied Republican voters, he could not be defeated because he rejected the policies of President George W. Bush. The 2016 election was an "Anti-George W. Bush" election.

"Time warps" are not frequent, but they do occur. We last faced a time warp in 1991 when the Soviet Union fell. Secretary of State James Baker couldn't think outside of the box and desperately wanted to secure relations with now-former Communist leaders of the Soviet Union. That administration could not adjust to the dramatic circumstances that changed the balance of power overnight. Despite James Baker's reputation as a "realist," so contented was he with relations with the Soviet Union before 1991 that he could not adjust his thinking to a new balance of power that had occurred with the collapse of Soviet communism. An opportunity was lost to restructure NATO, release responsibility for the defense of Western Europe to the Western Europeans, and pare back the administrative state with tax cuts and reduced government spending.

Time warps tend to block our vision of new and powerful forces which, in the American electorate today, include new generations of young voters who feel that the system is rigged against them, that their votes are useless, and that programs enacted since the New Deal and Great Society will deprive them of the middle-class comforts enjoyed by their parents and deny them a secure retirement.

Chapter 4

Fr. Stanley Parry, CSC, & Gerhart Niemeyer

Modern American intellectual conservatism is spiritually akin to the rebellion symbolized in the "Spirit of '76." But, instead of the limitations of Enlightenment reasoning unsympathetic to Christianity that adversely affected some of the 18th-century American colonial leaders like Thomas Jefferson, many modern conservatives were fortunate to participate in, and become the beneficiaries of, a recovery of classical Greek philosophy. That philosophy, which was open to the divine presence in reality, enabled us to reconcile our reason with our religious experience.

That was the "home" where I found myself in the winter of 1965, astonished that I was soon to attend a seminar on Modern Political Theory with Eric Voegelin, a seminar on Communist Ideology with Gerhart Niemeyer, and a seminar with Fr. Stanley Parry, CSC, on St. Augustine and Thomas Hobbes.

We mid-20th-century conservative students, fortunate enough to enroll in Notre Dame's graduate program in Government, understood that we were given the opportunity of recovering the wisdom, foresight, and prudence of the Founding Fathers who shaped the constitution of the United States and of integrating philosophical truth into our defense of tradition.

Beginning in the 1960s, we saw how Enlightenment symbols of rights, equality, and liberty became autonomous from the rule of law and were used as pretexts for New Left license and nihilism. It has taken my generation of conservatives fifty years to recover the intellectual ground that enables us today to articulate a way to recovery of political order.

We modern conservatives were forced to fashion new intellectual ground to support ordered liberty against the onslaught of modern ideologies at home and totalitarianism abroad. During the 20th Century, perhaps the bloodiest in the history of mankind, East, Central and Western Europe had been subjected to revolutions and a succession of wars that destroyed the Austro-Hungarian, Russian, German, and Ottoman empires. The descent into a frenzy of madness and destruction in East and Central Europe led, little more than a quarter century later, to a second World War and saw the occupation of France and the survival of England seriously threatened.

When monarchies were overthrown and replaced with totalitarian regimes, the United States was compelled to fight a succession of wars from World War II and the Korean War to the war in Vietnam. Nothing grows more quickly during war than the powers of the State with the result that, by the end of the 20th Century, the American administrative state had become the enemy of all Americans, but only social, political, and economic conservatives seemed concerned.

In the United States, the intellectual recovery that was required to analyze and resolve the threat to American freedom from the administrative state took place both at Notre Dame under the influence of Eric Voegelin, Gerhart Niemeyer, and Fr. Stanley Parry, CSC, and at the University of Chicago under the influence of Leo Strauss.

Two works that symbolize that recovery are Eric Voegelin's *The New Science of Politics* and Leo Strauss's *Natural Right and History.*

At Notre Dame, my new "home," under the tutelage of Eric Voegelin, Gerhart Niemeyer, and Fr. Stanley Parry, CSC, and later Ralph McInerny, was an invitation to metamorphose into something entirely different from that which I had been—a metamorphosis into something I did not even know existed.

As an undergraduate at the University of Pittsburgh, I had worked for the county Republican Party, pursued the role of a conservative activist on campus, worked on the Nixon and Goldwater campaigns for president, and plotted a future political career in Pennsylvania.

Had I pursued that course, my career would undoubtedly have included law school and a successful run for the Pennsylvania state legislature and, probably, a criminal indictment.

Politics in my hometown of Pittsburgh, like throughout the Commonwealth of Pennsylvania, was thoroughly corrupt. Jim Malone shared with me his consternation that sitting judges took retainers from their former law firms; voter registration lists and voting machines were rigged; voters were bribed for votes; and members of the state legislature supplemented their income with bribes. By the grace of God, I was intellectually curious, even anxious, to find answers to fundamental questions about the intellectual confusion of the historical moment in which I lived and, frankly, the ignorance of the American electorate who voted for the Kennedy presidency, which was soon to come to a disastrous and tragic end.

I was compelled to satisfy a thirst to comprehend what it was that created the historical predicament of the Cold War and the willingness by both political parties to grow the powers of an American government which I believed threatened to doom my country to despotism.

At the University of Pittsburgh, few shared my judgment that the United States had not responded to the challenge of the Soviet Union in Cuba and Berlin and that the United States was a nation in peril, and no one told me that a course of intellectual recovery existed. My behaviorist professors in psychology, liberal professors in political science, and Marxist graduate assistants in the Department of History were representatives of a deformed consciousness, not the solution to a spiritual disease that infected our intellectual classes who were ignorant of the fact that they were ignorant.

The intellectual challenge that I encountered at Notre Dame, therefore, opening the doors to classical philosophy as it did, challenged me to understand the originating experiences that led to the development of philosophy in ancient Greece. Recovery of classical philosophy was in process in the writings of my political theory teachers at Notre Dame, namely Eric Voegelin, Gerhart Niemeyer, and Fr. Stanley Parry, CSC.

They had done my homework for me, had plowed the road, but left me alone to travel in the direction that road went. What they discovered could not be reduced to propositions but required that I live a life of analysis, contemplation, and reflection. I had them as an example and could follow in their footsteps, but the task ahead would be far more consuming than I had any reason to comprehend when I first arrived in South Bend.

After making that journey of 380 miles from Pittsburgh, Pennsylvania, to South Bend, Indiana, I could not return to where I had been born and raised and simply pick up life where I left it. Perhaps "chosen" is too strong a word to describe that I was about to set course on an intellectual journey deep into the recesses of the human soul and mind, of human history and artifacts of ancient civilizations, and there to recover experiences of reality that had been occluded by American secular culture. Whatever term describes that, I know that this course which I chose was best for me.

During the years that followed, I began to learn how to interpret those experiences, analyze the present historical moment, and apply that experience to a political philosophy that would outline the limits of state power. This was political theory, not conservative political theory, but identifying freedoms threatened by our administrative state placed us in opposition to those who wanted that state apparatus to grow in beneficent powers, programs, and policies. Saying that this couldn't be done made us conservative.

That was the burden carried by the students of Eric Voegelin, Gerhart Niemeyer, and Fr. Stanley Parry, CSC, three men who were participating in the recovery of the philosophical basis of the West. Of these three, only Fr. Stanley Parry, CSC, was a Catholic, and the irony of that ecumenical event never fails to amaze me.

In following a philosophic path under Voegelin's, Niemeyer's, and Fr. Parry's guidance, I discovered that my spiritual life and my intellectual life were not contrary to one another but traveled along parallel courses to equivalent experience. And I would later apply these truths to American politics, constitutional history, and the history of American political thought.

In an America fast becoming completely secularized and dominated by an expansive, spiritually diminished, bureaucratic administrative state, I was fortunate enough to encounter the one American school of political philosophy in my lifetime that was open to the divine presence in reality.

At Notre Dame, in that moment in time, in the recesses of the Department of Government in the throes of being remaindered by a Catholic Church rushing toward a cultural crackup, our teachers pursued truth without impairment by the acid of skepticism, ideology, and dogmatism and were sowing the seeds of a political renaissance that in 2015 I came to call the Conservative Rebellion.[1]

From left: William F. Buckley, Jr., and Gerhart Niemeyer

So, twenty years after the end of World War II, I was fortunate to find myself in the bowels of one of America's

---

[1] Richard Bishirjian, *The Conservative Rebellion* (South Bend, IN: St. Augustine's Press, 2015).

premier Catholic educational institutions where there remained a few émigré European scholars who had been part
of the diaspora from totalitarian movements that had destroyed Western, Central and Eastern Europe, and Russia.
Learning the fundamentals of classical political philosophy
from two Protestants and one Catholic priest was clearly an
exception in American higher education.

Contrary to the indoctrination that was going on around
them at American colleges and universities, these classical
philosophers gave me free reign to unleash my desire to grow
in my studies without impediment by a developing Left
University.[2]

Though it is not necessary to state this, while at odds with
the criticism leveled at conservative scholarship by the Left,
I was neither learning doctrine nor becoming a conservative
activist under the tutelage of these three men. I was being
encouraged to take on the adult responsibility of "existence
in truth"[3] of classical philosophy with all my intellect.

At the beginning of this effort to recall those days in my
new "home," I knew it would be very difficult—for me at

---

[2] James Piereson, "The Left University: How it was born; how
it grew; how to overcome it," *The Weekly Standard*, Vol. 11, Issue
3 (October 3, 2005). Available online at
https://www.washingtonexaminer.com/weekly-standard/the-left-
university

[3] Eric Voegelin, *On Debate and Existence*, p. 36.

least—since the works of Eric Voegelin, Gerhart Niemeyer, and Fr. Stanley Parry, CSC, are not suitable for compiling lists of their ideas.

They asked and attempted to answer the great questions of the Western philosophical tradition: "What is order?" "What is right by nature?" "What is tradition?" "What is ideology?" "What is history?" "What is philosophy?" "What is nature?"[4] A part of my education required that I understand why these questions were important and had to be asked. All these, and more, were subjects of philosophical inquiry under their tutelage. And I had so very much to learn, so many things to read, so many languages to study and, I thought, so little time.

Gerhart Niemeyer taught a concentrated yearlong graduate course entitled "Communist Ideology" that required us to read most of the works of Marx and Engels, Lenin, Stalin, Mao Tse-tung, and the major Communist Party pronouncements. Niemeyer also taught two undergraduate courses. The first was entitled "Modern Ideology" in which we read the histories of medieval millennialism and the texts of Manicheans and ancient Gnostics, texts that enabled us to experience the decadence in their literature. That was followed by the second course on the recovery of political

---

[4] Bradley Lewis, "Life and Work of Gerhart Niemeyer," Phoenix Institute Summer Seminar for the Study of Western Institutions, University of Notre Dame (1 July 2010).

theory anchored in Voegelin's works, Albert Camus's *The Rebel*, Henri Bergson's *The Two Sources Of Morality And Religion*, and the studies in comparative religion of Mircea Eliade.

Gerhart Niemeyer

Niemeyer taught two additional seminars with a focus on the concept of nature and the concept of history where we necessarily became absorbed in the basic texts of the major philosophers who had addressed those subjects.

Fr. Stanley Parry, CSC, taught seminars on the history of political theory, classical and modern. In my first semester, I had the opportunity to read St. Augustine and Thomas Hobbes under his tutelage.

Eric Voegelin taught whatever he wanted to teach under the rubrics of modern and classical political theory. I took his seminar entitled "Modern Political Theory," audited his undergraduate political theory class, and attended his lectures on revolution and other subjects. Since Voegelin lived on campus and dined in the cafeteria, my colleagues and I would join him for dinner and continue discussions we began in class.

My research with Ralph McInerny on the early Greek natural philosophers shaped my understanding of the conflict between Homeric myth and ancient Greek religion and the new consciousness of the Greek tragedians and natural philosophers.

Coming to Notre Dame midyear in the academic calendar after working in the 1964 Goldwater campaign, I was required to introduce myself to Professor Niemeyer and be approved to enroll in his course on Communist Ideology midway through by reading Lenin without having the benefit of a semester's reading of Marx and Engels. Sitting with me in his small office, Niemeyer wanted to know why I was entering graduate school now and not with everyone else in September. I didn't hesitate, but I was uncomfortable telling him that I had worked on a losing presidential campaign. When I admitted what so many of my professors had considered reprehensible, Niemeyer's voice softened, and he invited me to dinner at his home. My graduate student colleagues were stunned. "Niemeyer never invites students to his home."

With Fr. Parry's seminar on St. Augustine, I began my interest in the wonderful mind of this Catholic saint. I hope that when I die, I will have an opportunity to meet this great Christian and to continue my education at his feet.

Voegelin's seminar on Modern Political Theory was also a challenge since I lacked the tools of classical philosophy. And my foreign language training was deficient. I had to make up what I should have begun in secondary school and college by studying Latin, Classical Greek, and German, before completing my doctoral dissertation. Later, I added Sanskrit, the language of the Hindu religion and of the philosophy found in the Upanishads.

I enjoyed every moment that I was at Notre Dame, but until I stepped onto the tarmac at South Bend airport in January, 1965, I had never read a word of the pre-Socratics, Plato, Aristotle, or St. Augustine. At the University of Pittsburgh, my education, except in the English literature courses that I took, started in the 19th century and ended in behaviorist political science that was the "rage" in higher education in the 1960s.

Though Fr. Parry's seminar on Thomas Hobbes and St. Augustine was the first and only course that I took with him, a fellow graduate student and I journeyed to Chicago with him in February, 1965, to attend the first meetings of The Philadelphia Society.[5] That gave us the opportunity to spend

---

[5] Audio recordings of this first conference of The Philadelphia Society (held on February 26-27, 1965, at the Sheraton-Chicago)

personal time with him and brought us into close proximity with leaders of a new and exciting conservative intellectual community of scholars.

Formed immediately after the 1964 election, The Philadelphia Society attracted all the major personalities whom we associate with modern conservatism, namely, Frank Meyer, Milton Friedman, Stephen Tonsor, Russell Kirk, Stefan Possony, Thomas Molnar, Robert Strausz-Hupé, Willmoore Kendall, L. Brent Bozell, and Gerhart Niemeyer. Being in the presence of these senior members of the conservative intellectual community inspired me to join them by completing my postgraduate degree program at Notre Dame.

Shortly after that seminar on Hobbes and St. Augustine, Fr. Parry left Notre Dame, experiencing disappointment and betrayal in being removed from his position of Chairman of the Department of Government. He left Notre Dame for Washington, D.C., where he conducted a project for William J. Baroody, Sr., founder of the American Enterprise Institute. His research was to lead to a study of Congressman Howard Smith (D-VA), powerful Chairman of the House Rules Committee. "Judge" Smith, who from 1955 to 1964 blocked passage of civil rights legislation, finally capitulated by releasing President Kennedy's civil rights legislation from the

---

are available online at https://phillysoc.org/tps_meetings/the-future-of-freedom-the-problems-and-the-prospects/

House Rules Committee. Later, I asked Fr. Parry what he discovered, and he said that Congressman Smith had cleaned
his files before he sent them to be archived. Thus, the evidence of what actually occurred when he released Kennedy's
legislation from the House Rules Committee was lost for-
ever. Fr. Parry next taught at the University of Dallas where
I took up my first teaching position as an Assistant Professor
of Politics. He was 54 years old when he died in 1972. He
once told me that the average age of Congregation of Holy
Cross priests buried in the cemetery at Notre Dame was 57.

Dr. John Gueguen's essay in *Logos* (2007)[6] succinctly
examines Fr. Parry's work and influence, gives a close reading of his analysis of Orestes Brownson, and discusses his
extraordinary collaboration with Gerhart Niemeyer in 1958
that led to a memorandum, which was published in Notre
Dame's *Scholastic* magazine, suggesting how the U.S.
government should address the issue of minority civil rights.

President Eisenhower had created the U.S. Commission
on Civil Rights in the fall of 1957, and the Parry/Niemeyer
memorandum outlined what can only be called a conservative approach to resolving "mutually exclusive concepts of
justice."[7] In light of the civil disturbances of the 1960s and
1970s associated with the civil rights movement, the clash

[6] John A. Gueguen, Jr., "Stanley Parry: Teacher and Prophet,"
Logos, Vol. 10, No. 2 (Spring 2007).
[7] Ibid., p. 7.

between state governments and the federal government, and the violence inflicted on demonstrators leading ultimately to the assassination of Martin Luther King, Jr., in 1968, Fr. Parry and Niemeyer were far ahead of events in calling for a constitutional structure that would assign to the government

> an all-embracing order of justice and constitutes a concept of the common good acceptable to groups with conflicting notions of justice. In other words, where people hold different and unreconciled ideas about justice, a limited function of the state is a moral duty. The state acts as an instrument of virtue precisely by refraining from acting as an instrument of salvation. It makes possible a peaceful and just community by confining itself to the peacemaking tasks of a reconciling constitutional structure.[8]

The Parry/Niemeyer memorandum argues that it is wrong for a government to "consider itself an instrument for the moral elevation or correction of groups of citizens," qualifying, however, that it is right for a government to "take authoritative action to protect the order of justice" by using

---

[8] "Politics and Morality in Civil Rights," *The Scholastic*, January 17, 1958, p. 12. This issue of the Scholastic may be accessed online at http://www.archives.nd.edu/Scholastic/VOL_0099/VOL_0099_ISSUE_0011.pdf

laws to educate people "to practice forbearance... in spite of disagreeing convictions and to subordinate partial interests to the common good."[9]

More than sixty years after publication of this memorandum, it still amazes me how prescient Fr. Parry and Niemeyer were and what their effort tells us about their own sense of public duty and their seeming knowledge that they, as representatives of the Government Faculty at the University of Notre Dame, spoke with some authority to a willing audience of similarly concerned citizens.

In fact, both Fr. Parry and Niemeyer had close ties to the Republican Party, the Eisenhower Administration and Bill Baroody's "think tank," the American Enterprise Institute, that presaged the relationship between the Reagan Administration and the Hoover Administration. Between the last year of the Eisenhower Administration and the election of President Reagan, everything that Fr. Parry and Niemeyer cautioned would occur did occur, and a twenty-year conservative rout removed common sense from American politics.

The damage done to American society, culture, and basic institutions by an aggressive administrative state during the decades of the '60s and '70s is something that we "Conservative Rebels" are compelled to overcome more than half a century later.

---

[9] Ibid., p. 13.

Fr. Parry's essay entitled "The Restoration of Tradition," published in *Modern Age* in the spring of 1961, remains his legacy.[10] What is tradition is an important problem in science. Fr. Parry begins his essay by identifying his subject as "paradigmatic" as opposed to "chronological" tradition. Paradigmatic history is measured by "the integrity of the original compact experience of truth whose differentiation constitutes the stages of the history."[11] Within the context of that meaning, he defines tradition as "nothing more than the concrete experience of truth carried distributively and in common by a multitude whom the experience unites and structures for action in pragmatic history."[12] This tradition is important because it completes us as citizens and as human beings living in society. A "sense of communion" with truth that arises in this social setting is "tradition." He writes, "For above all, tradition exists as the experience of truth."[13] That truth, he finds, is "the common good."

The modern dilemma that Fr. Parry addresses in his essay is the descent from truth to falsehood when contemporary events "replace the real experience of truth with un-

---

[10] Stanley Parry, "The Restoration of Tradition," *Modern Age* (Spring 1961). This essay may be accessed online at https://isi.org/modern-age/the-restoration-of-tradition/

[11] Ibid., p. 126.

[12] Ibid., p. 126.

[13] Ibid., p. 126.

real images of it."[14] Fr. Parry identifies the contest between liberals and conservatives as representative of a change in tradition that "involves a diminution in the intensity of communally experienced truth—in consensus—and a falling out of the area of experience large segments of previously held truth."[15] This type of change "is not a change from one positive position to another, but a change from order and truth to disorder and negation."[16]

Living in a society in which tradition is contested is the bane of contemporary America, and though we experience discomfort and are ill at ease in daily life, Fr. Parry suggests that something more, even dangerous, is at work. In societies that experience a loss of tradition, a change from order to disorder occurs that "works itself out as a disruption of the individual soul, a change in which man continues as an objective ontological existent, but no longer as a man."[17] As the character of the nation changes for the worse, we move toward a condition of loss of our humanity!

A few years ago, a former student told me, "I can no longer recognize my country." That is symptomatic of the dissolution of tradition and "the isolation of an ideational exis-

---

[14] Ibid., p. 127.
[15] Ibid., p. 127.
[16] Ibid., p. 128.
[17] Ibid., p. 129.

tence in the minds of unrelated individuals."[18] Ideas now gain importance not as "the form of society" but as "goals of creative action."[19] That is accompanied by an increase in the role of government in imposing those ideas and the absence of "theoretical argument" about their truth.

In anticipation of some contemporary conservative responses to our current disorders, Fr. Parry suggests that the responses of "economic individualism" and "spiritual individualism" are insufficient. Laissez-faire capitalism's economic response to collectivism is inadequate because it is based solely in economics. Those who identify society itself as the villain won't find a solution in "the realm of the individual's return to truth by paths sometimes solitary and stern."[20]

Fr. Parry admits that he himself does not have the answer to our current crisis. Fortunately, he writes, similar crises have occurred at least twice, once during the collapse of the Greek city-state and again at the collapse of the Roman empire. Both generated restorative responses, that of Plato and that of St. Augustine, and each response is prophetic, requiring "the attempt to restore tradition to its ontological status as the form of society."[21] The recovery process is made difficult because the criticism brought to the analysis of the

---

[18] Ibid., p. 131.

[19] Ibid., p. 132.

[20] Ibid., p. 134.

[21] Ibid., p. 136.

disorder will discover that "the principle in which disolution [sic] originates is itself part of the tradition."[22] When, and if, some semblance of a prophetic response to the crisis appears, it "must ultimately express itself as a new interpretation of history itself in which the break, the dissolution, becomes part of a larger pattern of purpose."[23]

My encounter with Gerhart Niemeyer at Notre Dame was also life-changing. My first meeting with him was memorable. It took place in his office in January, 1965, and throughout that semester, I struggled to comprehend the content of the second course in a two-course series entitled Communist Ideology. At the end of that semester, Niemeyer arranged an internship for me at Georgetown University's Center for Strategic Studies with his former student, Richard V. Allen. I returned to Notre Dame in September, 1965, and completed Niemeyer's course on History and Political Order and the first part of his seminar on Communist Ideology.

In January, 1966, feeling deficient in classical Latin and Greek, I took a leave of absence to enroll in a concentrated Latin program at Loyola University of Chicago and a summer introduction to classical Greek at Hunter College. I returned to Notre Dame in the fall of 1966 and served two years as Niemeyer's graduate teaching assistant while also completing his seminar entitled Concepts of Nature.

---

[22] Ibid., p. 136.

[23] Ibid., p. 137.

In the fall of 1968, I left Notre Dame to attend classes with Michael Oakeshott at the London School of Economics and to work on my doctoral dissertation on Thomas Carlyle and 19th-Century Gnosticism.[24] I returned to the United States in the fall of 1969 to teach in the Politics Department at the University of Dallas.

In 1970, Niemeyer visited the University of Dallas where, in typical Niemeyer fashion,[25] he expressed concern that my dissertation was not on track. Such encounters, few as they were, had an immediate effect. I rectified my errors and completed the work for graduation with my Ph.D. early in 1971.

Niemeyer's life has been summarized by Walter Nicgorski,[26] Michael Henry,[27] and Bruce Fingerhut,[28] and

---

[24] See Richard Bishirjian, "Carlyle's Political Religion," *The Journal of Politics*, Vol. 38, No. 1 (Feb., 1976), 95-113.

[25] Angelo Codevilla compares Niemeyer's concerns as similar to a "Baltic breeze." Angelo Codevilla, "Thank You, Gerhart Niemeyer," University Bookman, 5.5.2013.

[26] Walter Nicgorski, "Politics, Political Philosophy, and Christian Faith: Gerhart Niemeyer's Journey" *The Political Science Reviewer*, Vol. 31 (July, 2002), 41-69. Available online at https://politicalsciencereviewer.wisc.edu/index.php/psr/article/view/410

[27] Michael Henry, ed., *The Loss and Recovery of Truth: Selected Writings of Gerhart Niemeyer* (South Bend, IN: St. Augustine's Press, 2013).

[28] Bruce Fingerhut, *Look for the Lift: A Biographical Essay of Gerhart Niemeyer*, in A Symposium on Gerhart Niemeyer, ed.

others. Bruce Fingerhut's summary places Niemeyer's life in
historical context:

> Born February 15, 1907, in Essen, Germany, Gerhart
> Niemeyer was educated at Cambridge (1925-1926),
> Munich (1926-1927) and Kiel (1927-1930), where he
> received a J.U.D. in 1932. He left Germany in 1933 and
> joined friend and mentor, Hermann Heller, in Madrid,
> Spain. His career as a teacher began as a lecturer at the
> University of Madrid in 1933–1934 and assistant pro-
> fessor at the Institute for International and Economic
> Studies in Madrid in 1934–1936. In 1936, he left Madrid
> for what was to be a brief vacation. A week later, the
> Spanish Civil War erupted, preventing his return to the
> Institute. He emigrated to the United States in 1937,
> becoming a citizen in 1943, and began teaching at
> Princeton (until 1944) and Oglethorpe (1944-1950). He
> served as visiting professor at Yale (1942, 1946, 1954-
> 1955) and Columbia (1952).[29]

Here the intervention of Fr. Parry in 1955 was critical,
for his desire to bring Gerhart Niemeyer to the Department

Michael Henry, *The Political Science Reviewer*, Vol. XXXI, 2002.
This essay may be accessed online at
http://www.firstprinciplesjournal.com/articles.aspx?article=1596
[29] Ibid.

of Government at Notre Dame required the approval of Notre Dame's president, Fr. Theodore Hesburgh. Fr. Parry accumulated letters of recommendation and sent them to the president's office over a series of weeks. Finally, Hesburgh gave his assent. That assured that Niemeyer's intellectual quest would be based in a supportive institution. No outline of Niemeyer's life, however, can inform those who did not know him of his personal gravitas.

In every life, men and women may be fortunate once or twice to encounter someone who turns us around or redirects our lives in ways that make all the difference. Gerhart Niemeyer was such a person.

His entry into my life, and into the lives of his biographers cited above, begins with his appointment in 1955. The University of Notre Dame is one of several Catholic Universities that has made major contributions to American politics, scholarship, religion, and science. But, Notre Dame, for at least two decades from 1955 to 1975, was unique in that it was open to seminal work in political theory by Notre Dame's Department of Government's Fr. Stanley Parry, CSC, Gerhart Niemeyer, and Eric Voegelin.

Niemeyer and Fr. Parry were the anchors that held the accomplishments of these three scholars in a dynamic relationship with their students. I personally mark the fifty years since the removal of Fr. Stanley Parry as Chairman of the Department of Government as the commencement of Notre Dame's decline into a secular university. But for a brief period—more than enough time to launch the careers of many of the political theorists we associate with the recovery of classical political theory in America—Notre Dame was the place to study political philosophy. If that statement is true, its truth may be traced to the influence of Gerhart Niemeyer.

My appointment as Niemeyer's Teaching Assistant was also formative and required that I learn how to grade papers and exams of undergraduate students in his History of Political Theory class. That course was required of Government majors, and I was assigned to teach the 8:00 am section of his class that met on Saturday mornings. Though one might assume that 8:00 am on a Saturday would not attract many students, in fact, my class session was full of students who wanted to avoid preparing for the likelihood that Niemeyer would call on them to explain that week's reading assignment.

Like Fr. Parry, Gerhart Niemeyer's influence did not depend on the books he published, though these include his early work, *Law Without Force* (1941), *An Inquiry into Soviet Mentality* (1956), *The Communist Ideology* (Vol. I of *Facts on Communism*, 1959), *Handbook on Communism* (edited with J. M. Bochenski, 1962), *An Outline of Communism* (1966), *Deceitful Peace* (1971), *Between Nothingness and Paradise* (1971), *Aftersight and Foresight* (1988), and *Within and Above Ourselves* (1996).

Niemeyer, like everyone born in the 20th century, lived in interesting times that shaped his life's work. Faced with the threat of an international communist movement fueled by a Russian nation captured by the Bolsheviks, Americans knew little to nothing about communism, the nature of "ideology," and the revolutionary agenda of the Soviet Union. And the ignorance of a president of the United States in his relations with the Soviet Union during World War II could easily have ended with the death of freedom in the West.[30]

What Americans did know about communism was false, that Stalin was a reformer much like the reformers of the New Deal. That ignorance led to the start of a Cold War.

Americans, like the ancient Romans, are a practical people. We are doers not thinkers, and unlike the ancient Greeks, philosophy does not come to us easily. Thus, faced with a regime governed by an ideological program of world domination, it was simply too difficult for most Americans to understand the nature of the threat.

Gerhart Niemeyer devoted a significant portion of his professional career to making it known among his fellow Americans what the Communist threat was, what its intentions were, and how and why those ideological principles were aimed at the heart of the Christian West.

Five of the books in his curriculum vitae are focused on communism. And his students in the graduate program in

---

[30] M. Stanton Evans and Herbert Romerstein, *Stalin's Secret Agents: The Subversion of Roosevelt's Government* (New York: Threshold Editions, 2013).

Government at Notre Dame were initiated into communist ideology through an intensive program of required reading of, literally, every work of Marx, Engels, Lenin, Stalin, the Communist Party of the Soviet Union, and Mao Tse-tung. How difficult that was for me and for many others in Niemeyer's two-semester course series can only be measured by our later relief when the Soviet Union collapsed in 1991, and we no longer had to study the ideas of that regime.

I must have learned something, however, since the first and only time I taught a course on communist ideology in 1975, I was pleasantly surprised by the interest of my students in learning about this ideology and how quickly they discerned the threat it presented to our "bourgeois" concepts of freedom. After completing that course, they might be seduced by liberal politicians, but not by communists.

Niemeyer's *Between Nothingness and Paradise* (1971), the collection of his essays published in *Aftersight and Foresight* (1988), and the comprehensive, 669-page collection of essays compiled and edited by Michael Henry in *The Loss and Recovery of Truth: Selected Writings of Gerhart Niemeyer* (2013) are the primary resources for contemporary students who desire to learn something about him.

As with Eric Voegelin, it is not possible to summarize Niemeyer's political philosophy in a few paragraphs. Like the important scholars he admired, namely Eric Voegelin, Henri Bergson, Albert Camus, Mircea Eliade, Hans Jonas, J. L.

Talmon, Norman Cohn, Robert Nisbet, and many others, Niemeyer was engaged in studying problems in science.

The "total critique" of reality that Niemeyer examines in *Between Nothingness and Paradise* gives insights into the science of totalitarianism which, following Albert Camus, he understood is a "metaphysical rebellion."[31]

The seduction of the West by totalitarian movements did not occur overnight, however. There was a "long period of intellectual erosion preceding the advent of the activists."[32] The West was, after a fashion, softened up by humanist intellectuals going as far back as the 17th-century Enlightenment thinkers.

Understanding totalitarian political regimes begins with "the denial and destruction of ontological foundations of order," as Niemeyer wrote,

> The quality that we designate by the word 'total' applies to totalitarian movements not because they invade what had until then been a 'private' sphere of action, but because they aim beyond mere structural change at the denial and destruction of ontological foundations of order. A totalitarian movement acts in a society as a dissolvent of the xynon (Heraclitus), the common awareness of the bonds between political order and the nature

---

[31] Gerhart Niemeyer, *Between Nothingness and Paradise* (Baton Rouge: Louisiana State University Press, 1971), p. 143.
[32] Ibid.

of being. Where and insofar as the totalitarian attack is crowned by success, it destroys not merely institutions and powerholders but the transpositive guidance of laws, as well as the order by which families and individual persons live.[33]

Niemeyer's analysis was supported by personal experience. *From Europe, With Love*, from the collection of Niemeyer essays, *The Loss and Recovery of Truth*, relates an incident in Germany, when the outbreak of the Spanish Civil War blocked his return to Spain, that serves to explain how totalitarian rule destroys personal order.

One afternoon, while taking a walk, I met a little 4-year old girl who greeted me with, "Heil Hitler", and I returned the greeting "Good afternoon". Back from my walk two hours later, I found my landlady in a state of alarm. The police had been there, inquiring about me and my political orientation. When asked why the inquiry, they said I had failed to use the Nazi salute.[34]

---

[33] Ibid., p. 140.

[34] Gerhart Niemeyer, "From Europe, With Love," in Michael Henry, ed., *The Loss and Recovery of Truth*, p. 8.

Niemeyer's investigation of totalitarian ideology reveals both "axiological" and "praxiological" aspects of the denial of reality.

Axiological denial of reality manifests itself in the speculative assertion of a good opposed to the goodness found in the historical world. "[M]an's historical existence is seen as essentially separated from his true reality."[35] The "truth" of the totalitarian is wholly speculative, grounded in the will and imaginative creation of a future reality, opposed to the present, of the ideologue.

The praxiological aspect pulls the norms of an imagined reality into the real world and organizes human action according to the false reality. Following Albert Camus, Niemeyer distinguished between a "total critique of society" and "rebellion," which is directed at specific injustices. The Greek word for "being" is *on*, and Niemeyer describes the total critique as a form of "ontophobia"—fear of being—that he indicates is similar to the ancient Gnostics' obsession with an evil demiurge, or God, who trapped the divine spark in the man of the material world.

> This similarity is found in metaphysical discontent, the attribution of evil to the environing world rather than to the human heart, belief in the possibility of salvation from the evil world as a whole, certainty that salvation is

---

[35] Niemeyer, *Between Nothingness and Paradise*, p. 141.

to be wrought by human action, and the acceptance of ideological 'knowledge' of the method of total change as the message of salvation for mankind.[36]

Here Niemeyer speaks of an antidote to metaphysical rebellion in a "philosophy of limits." The concept is Albert Camus's for whom, "There does exist for man… a way of acting and thinking which is possible on the level of moderation to which he belongs… Politics is not religion."[37] Niemeyer observes that "For Camus, this way of acting and thinking consists in rebellion, a negative affirmation in which he sees the establishment of a common human dignity."[38]

Between Nothingness and Paradise ends with three chapters that are offered as an antidote to the totalitarian temptation. Like so many theoretical formulations of great significance—one thinks of Aristotle's few paragraphs on "right by nature" or St. Augustine's distinction between the City of Man and the City of God—Niemeyer's analysis in chapters entitled *Past, Future, and Present*; *The Ethics of Existence*; and *True and False Prophets* are 82 pages of compact

---

[36] Ibid., 142.

[37] Albert Camus, *The Rebel: An Essay on Man in Revolt*. Trans. by Anthony Bower. (New York City: Alfred A. Knopf, Inc., 1956), p. 302.

[38] Ibid., 143.

theoretical reflection about the reality of community, continuity of peoples in history, the origin of community in theophanous experience, and what Niemeyer calls "history as a mode of existence."

This mention of 'theophany' requires that we attempt to explain what has been obscured by the loss of philosophy or, better said, its replacement with the influence of British empiricism. All that we really know, Locke argued, is based in sense experience.[39] With that one assertion, all non-material reality was banned from educated conversation. Yet an intelligent observer, William James, as early as 1901, had recovered an understanding that there is a world of "varieties" of "religious experience." Theophany is a religious experience of non-material reality, of the sacred, of something "other," that is not part of the world of immanent things.

Some passages from these 82 pages resonate for those of his students who took his seminar entitled "History and Political Order" or assisted him in his undergraduate "History of Political Theory" course. In the History and Political Order seminar, we had fourteen weeks to study some of the works cited here, including Eric Voegelin's *Order and History*; Aristotle's *Nicomachean Ethics*; the books of Exodus, Deuteronomy, and Ecclesiastes; St. Augustine's *City of God* and his *Confessions*; Mircea Eliade's *The Myth of the Eternal*

---

[39] John Locke, *An Essay Concerning Human Understanding*, II.20.2.

Return; Manlius Severinus Boethius' *Consolation of Philosophy*; Giambattista Vico's *New Science*; Ibn Khaldûn's *Muqaddimah*; and Albert Camus's *The Rebel*.

Chapter 5

Eric Voegelin

My encounter with Eric Voegelin spanned the years 1965 to 1980. It commenced my first semester at Notre Dame in January 1965 and continued during a semester that Voegelin was in residence at Notre Dame in 1967, during a semester Voegelin spent at the University of Dallas in 1971, and at the Vanderbilt Conference on Gnosticism and Modernity that I organized with John William Corrington and William Havard in 1978. In 1980, I visited Voegelin and his wife one last time while attending a meeting of the Mont Pèlerin Society at Stanford University in Palo Alto. Eric Voegelin died in January 1985.

For many great scholars, teaching is an extension of research, and Voegelin would use his classes to expound on subjects about which he was writing at the time. I was fortunate to be in his class when he was writing his essay on immortality and dealing with the primacy of experience in classic philosophy. This was shortly before publication of Volume Four of *Order and History, The Ecumenic Age*, and just after publication of *Anamnesis*.

In his graduate classes at the University of Dallas in 1971, which I sometimes attended, Voegelin was asked by his students to read from Volume Two of *Order and History* those passages dealing with the origin of philosophy in the pre-Socratics. His students were so enthralled by Voegelin, and hungry for understanding classical philosophy, that they forced Voegelin to take something he had written two decades earlier and use that as the text of his seminar.

So, what was all the fuss? What was Voegelin teaching that instilled awe and inspiration in me and these students?

His focus on man's experience of reality and, especially, man's experience of transcendent divine reality, amazement at existence, and recovery of classical philosophy were the essential ingredients of his appeal. In contrast, the dominant academic approach asserted that all things are relative, neither true nor false, and that, therefore, the wisdom litera-ture which shaped the West was mere opinion.

Voegelin's first three volumes of *Order and History* revealed his "philosophical anthropology," an approach that was deeply historical and analytic that explored the artifacts and textual evidence of ancient cultures by interpreting the symbols by which human communities express their con-sciousness of order. His first volume in *Order and History*, entitled *Israel and Revelation*, is a masterful interpretation of the experience of Yahweh's revelation of Himself to the ancient Hebrew clans and Yahweh's Covenant with Israel that differentiated Israel from the cosmological empires of the ancient Near East.

My friend, John William Corrington,[1] told me that he found Volume One of *Order and History* while browsing the stacks in the library at Tulane University, and when he returned home, Corrington told his wife, "By God, he's done it!" What Voegelin had done in Volume One of *Order and History*, and which excited Corrington upon first reading it, was to give scholarly affirmation to Christian faith by identifying and interpreting the symbols that articulated the experience of revelation recorded in the Old Testament. So deep had the acid of relativism and nihilism seeped into American intellectual culture that Corrington's encounter with Voegelin shocked him.

Many of us who were attracted to Voegelin's political philosophy appreciated its compatibility with our Christian faith. For the first time in our intellectual journey, we could explore philosophy without the acid of skepticism, atheism, and political religion blocking our philosophical search.

Like most professors, Voegelin used materials in his courses that would later appear in his published works. I

---

[1] John William Corrington (1932-1988) was a novelist, a literary critic, a script writer for television and motion pictures, a legal scholar, an attorney, a philosopher, and a professor of English. See https://www.centenary.edu/academics/departments-schools/english/corrington-award

encountered his seminal insights before they were published within the classes that he taught at Notre Dame from 1965 to 1968. During that period, he published *Anamnesis* (1966)[2] and *The Ecumenic Age* (1974).[3] Some of his lectures developed themes that appeared later in important essays,[4] such as "What is Nature?, What is Right by Nature?, Reason: The Classic Experience,"[5] "On Debate and Existence,"[6] "Immortality: Experience and Symbol,"[7] "The Eclipse of Reality,"[8] "The Gospel and Culture,"[9] "Equivalences of Experience and

---

[2] In *The Collected Works of Eric Voegelin*, Vol. 6 (Columbia, MO: University of Missouri Press, 2002). Also, Gerhart Niemeyer trans. (South Bend: University of Notre Dame Press, 1978).

[3] In *The Collected Works of Eric Voegelin*, Vol. 4 (Columbia, MO: University of Missouri Press, 2000).

[4] In *Published Essays: 1966-1985, The Collected Works of Eric Voegelin, Vol. 12* (Louisiana State University Press, 1990).

[5] In *Southern Review*, Vol. 13, No. 5.

[6] In *Intercollegiate Review*, Vol. 3, Number 4-5 (March-April, 1967), pp. 143-152.

[7] In *Harvard Theological Review*, LX (1967), pp. 235-279.

[8] Unpublished essay c. 1969, in *The Collected Works of Eric Voegelin*, Vol. 28 (Columbia, MO: University of Missouri Press, 1990), pp. 111-162.

[9] In *Jesus and Man's Hope*, Miller and Hadidian, eds., (Pittsburgh Theological Seminary Press, 1971), pp. 59-101.

Symbolization in History,"[10] "On Hegel: A Study in Sorcery"[11] and "On Classical Studies."[12]

Dr. Eric Voegelin

Lest I give the impression that Voegelin mostly focused on ancient Israel or Greek philosophy, I should report that he was a fountainhead of insight into contemporary studies that bore on his areas of interest and which dealt with similar problems, such as Frank Kermode's *Sense of an Ending* that explored man's experience of the limits of existence; Floyd Matson's *The Broken Image: Man, Science and Society*; R. D. Laing's *Divided* Self which Voegelin referred to in his ex-

---

[10] In *The Collected Works of Eric Voegelin*, Vol. 12 (Columbia, MO: University of Missouri Press, 1970), pp. 115-171.

[11] *Studium generale*, XXIV (1971), 335-368.

[12] *Modern Age*, Vol. 17, Number 1 (Winter 1973), pp. 2-8.

ploration of the similarity of modern philosophy to
schizophrenia; the analysis of "religion" and "faith" by
Wilfred Cantwell Smith; William James's examination of
religious experience in *Varieties of Religious Experience* that
oddly, he noted, had nothing to say about Greek philosophic
experience; Albert Camus's masterful study of revolution in
L'Homme Révolté (in English, *The Rebel*); and Michael
Oakeshott's classic introduction to Thomas Hobbes's
Leviathan. And, always, Voegelin would favorably cite
Bergson's *Two Sources of Morality and Religion*.

Eric Voegelin's "philosophical anthropology" is based on
analysis of the experience of the "open soul," a term coined
by Henri Bergson whose *Two Sources of Morality and
Religion* is an examination of the soul which is "open," not
self-centered, in its being transparent to the divine in its
unwilled erotic movement away from self-love. Men who
drew the multitude of mankind after them by their per-
suasive examples (one thinks of Moses, the prophets of
ancient Israel, Confucius, Socrates, Jesus of Nazareth) are
representative. Voegelin's philosophical anthropology, then,
is an examination of the historical event of the opening of
the soul in representative men and the consequences of their
consciousness of that movement for our understanding of
the order in the psyche of man, of history, and of society.
Voegelin writes, "The noetic luminosity of participation in
the movement of reality did not emerge in the history of
mankind before it emerged in the philosophers' own dif-

ferentiating acts."[13] That emerging truth can take thousands of years to develop as when the Greek natural philosophers began to question the myths that had sustained Hellenic culture since the second millennium BC.

The first classes of Voegelin's that I attended focused on the reality that there is experience and that the bedrock of experience, what he called "the Ground," cannot be refuted–only interpreted. In other words, reality *is*.

"Why is there something and not nothing?" "Why is something as it is, and not different?" These questions, first expressed by Leibniz in *Principes de la nature et de la grâce*,[14] fell upon me as if I had been hit by a load of bricks. Conditioned by the relativism of my former teachers, I failed to understand that the unease I experienced during my undergraduate education was the attraction of my soul to the Ground of reality and that I was being compelled to turn around from the unreality of my professors to reality. I would later read in Voegelin's 1974 essay "Reason: The Classic Experience," that "The unrest in a man's psyche may be luminous enough to understand itself as caused by ignorance concerning the ground and meaning of existence,

---

[13] Eric Voegelin, *Order and History*, Vol. 4, *The Ecumenic Age* (Baton Rouge: Louisiana State University Press, 1974), p. 217.

[14] Eric Voegelin, *On Debate and Existence*, p. 43.

so that the man will feel an active desire to escape from this state of ignorance... and to arrive at knowledge."[15]

The consciousness of the open soul, Voegelin wrote, is structured by noetic and pneumatic theophanies, experiences of divine reality which make up what can be called the "history of theophany."[16] Voegelin's discussion of a variety of theophanies, therefore, is critical to understanding his recovery of the philosophic quest from the spiritual dead end of the Enlightenment. Voegelin's *Order and History*, for example, and his later essays discussed here, explore the development of symbols of consciousness of theophany. Noetic theophany is an example. Though we often assume that translations of ancient works are sufficient, it helps to know the actual words that were used. *Nous* is the Greek word for "mind," but that translation cannot begin to express the depth of meaning conveyed by that word. Voegelin would remark how amazing was the opportunity of Plato and Aristotle to "map" the architecture of the soul, and in that effort, 'nous' was very important.

Nous is the highest capacity of the rational part of the soul and deals with "the highest objects of knowledge."[17] Aristotle sees the noetic contemplation of the divine as the

---

[15] Eric Voegelin, *Reason: The Classic Experience*, p. 270.

[16] Eric Voegelin, *The Ecumenic Age*, p. 252.

[17] Aristotle, *Nicomachean Ethics*, 1177a21.

striving to be deathless, or immortal, since *nous* is either "divine or the most divine thing in us."[18]

The discovery that the order of the soul is, in effect, the soul's openness to noetic experience is simultaneously the discovery of the soul's movement toward differentiated noetic consciousness. Voegelin writes that reality, as the philosophers came to understand it, "is not a static order of things given to a human observer once for all; it is moving, indeed, in the direction of emergent truth."[19] This "truth" of the philosophers is not a fixed piece of information, "but the event in which the process of reality becomes luminous to itself."[20] This "event" is historical in the sense that consciousness of history is a process shaped by theophanies.

History "is the In-Between where man responds to the divine presence and divine presence evokes the response of man."[21] The "In-Between" defines Voegelin's understanding of philosophy. We human beings are In-Between divine reality and the world of existing things, and our consciousness of order reflects that necessarily limited perspective.

The noetic discovery of the ancient Greeks was not the end of discovery of reality. In the experience of ancient Israel and in the Christian Gospels, we have a new event that is

---

[18] Aristotle, *Nicomachean Ethics*, 1177a16.

[19] Eric Voegelin, *The Ecumenic Age*, p. 217.

[20] Ibid., p. 186.

[21] Ibid., p. 242.

expressed in Voegelin's concept of "pneumatic." Pneuma, or spirit, is a concept used by Voegelin to distinguish between the philosopher's contemplative act and revelatory experience. The Ground is experienced in both the noetic and pneumatic opening of the soul. Voegelin explains that "[t]he two modes require two different types of language for their adequate expression. The immediate presence in the movements of the soul requires the revelatory language of consciousness."[22] Voegelin attempts to explain the difference between noetic and pneumatic experience of reality by reference to how divine reality is experienced. The divine is experienced from the direction of the "Beginning" and from the "Beyond."

The "Beyond" refers to Plato's symbol of experience of the transcendent Good beyond existence and essence which compels the soul in its movement away from the world of shadows and ignorance. As such, the "Beyond" is a symbol that articulates the experience of divine reality beyond the world of immanent existence. The experience of divine reality from the direction of a "Beginning" is symbolized in the language of cosmogonies which extend in their historical range from the cosmogonic myths of Egypt and Mesopotamia to the account of creation in Genesis and the formulation of the Gospel of John that "[i]n the beginning was the Word." Though God is revealed beyond the cosmos, "the

---

[22] Ibid., p. 63.

differentiation of existential truth does not abolish the cosmos in which the event occurs."[23]

Thus, in the Christian experience of the Gospel of John, the "Word" of the "Beginning" is identified with the Word of Christ who manifests the movement of the Word from the Beyond. In this manner, Voegelin identifies the equivalence of the reality experienced in philosophy with the reality experienced in the Gospels and does not accept the conventional opposition between reason and revelation.

Analyzed on the level of experience, noetic theophany articulates an aspect of the same divine reality expressed in the pneumatic symbols of Moses, the prophets, and the Gospels. "Faith in Christ," Voegelin writes, "means responsive participation in the same divine *pneuma* that was active in the Jesus who appeared in the vision [of St. Paul] as the Resurrected."[24] The noetic theophany of Plato is equivalent to the pneumatic theophany of St. Paul with this difference: the pneumatic theophany in the vision of St. Paul is marked by a further differentiation in the eschatological view of the immortality of man. Aristotle's observation that man strives through contemplation to become deathless[25] is given clarity in the Resurrection. Voegelin observes that this is not a matter of "Christological dogma." Paul's vision was "an

---

[23] Ibid., p. 53.

[24] Ibid., p. 242.

[25] *Nicomachean Ethics*, 1177a16.

event in metaleptic reality" that "emerges as a symbol from the Metaxy."[26]

The word *metalepsis*, literally translated as "participate," is found in Aristotle's *Metaphysics*[27] and is used extensively by Voegelin to explain that man participates in divine reality and thus is not the divine but exists in between. Our consciousness of participation in divine reality is not static.

Henri Bergson observed, for example, that the passage from the closed to the open soul is not an advance of degrees but a "sudden leap" into a different order of consciousness.[28] In *Order and History*, Voegelin has called this phenomenon a "leap-in-being"—those historical moments when a new truth about God and, in consequence, a fuller understanding of man and history is discovered. When a "leap-in-being" occurs,

---

[26] Eric Voegelin, *The Ecumenic Age*, p. 243.

[27] "And thought thinks on itself because it shares (metalepsin) the nature of the object of thought; for it becomes an object of thought in coming into contact with and thinking its objects, so that thought and object of thought are the same." Aristotle, *Metaphysica*, 1072b19f. *Metaphysica*, Second Edition, Vol. VIII. *The Works of Aristotle*, W. D. Ross, trans. (Oxford: At the Clarendon Press, 1963).

[28] Henri Bergson, *The Two Sources Of Morality And Religion*, R. Ashley Audra and Cloudesley Brereton, trans., 1935. (Doubleday Anchor), p. 73.

Not only will the unseemly symbols be rejected, but man will turn away from the world and society as the source of misleading analogy. He will experience a turning around, the Platonic *periagoge*, an inversion or conversion toward the true source of order. And this turning around, this conversion, results in more than an increase in knowledge concerning the order of being; it is a change in the order itself. For the participation in being changes its structure when it becomes emphatically a partnership with God, while the participation in mundane being recedes to second rank. The more perfect attunement to being through conversion is not an increase on the same scale but a qualitative leap. And when this conversion befalls a society, the converted community will experience itself as qualitatively different from all other societies that have not taken the leap.[29]

Such a qualitative spiritual eruption occurred when Israel discovered itself as a community of chosen people, living in the historical present under God. The ancient Israelites were conscious of themselves as having been taken up from among the other cultures. Their symbols were expressive of a compact consciousness of participation in being and they were made God's special people. In this sense, they

---

[29] Eric Voegelin, *Order and History (Volume 1): Israel and Revelation* (Louisiana State University Press, 1956), p. 10.

constituted a theopolity, or city of God, whose historical traditions began with a revelation of a transcendent God whose love for Israel as a people is visible in the history of ancient Israel. The historical consciousness of Israel did not remain static but became a stratum of historical consciousness which lay in the background of further development. In the Christian epoch, when the distinctions are more fully developed, as they were by St. Augustine, the history of Israel will become a phase in the *historia sacra*, in Church history, as distinguished from the profane history in which empires rise and fall. Hence, the emphatic partnership with God removes a society from the rank of profane existence and constitutes it as the representative of the *civitas Dei* in historical existence.[30]

Voegelin calls this process of movement, from compact to generalized insight, the process of "differentiation." Voegelin distinguishes between incomplete and complete breakthroughs or leaps-in-being. In Israel and Hellas, the breaks from the cosmological form were radical and complete, developing in their wake "pneumatic" and "poetic" symbols, respectively, which express the character of the theophanies which constituted the "leap." The cosmological civilization of the ancient Greeks was displaced as a consequence of the discovery of philosophy that transformed ex-

---

[30] Ibid., p. 10.

perience of man as a plaything of the gods into the source of order of society.

That insight, Voegelin called "macro-anthropos." Other societies, such as China, reveal only a partial or "tentative" breakthrough.[31] The concept of society as "macro-anthropos" occurs in China by a "leap-in-being" of the Confucian and Taoist sages, he writes, but the leap "was not radical enough to break the cosmological order completely."[32]

Voegelin's philosophical anthropology, consequently, goes beyond the traditional limits of political theory because political science itself is the outgrowth of a radical "leap-in-being," not a tentative one.

Voegelin saw that the history of order does not reveal an unremitting upward movement toward greater consciousness of being. The experience of the open soul is sometimes deformed. The general term which Voegelin gives to the eclipse of experiential symbols is "derailment." Derailment can occur to any symbolism, in any experiential mode. The cosmological symbol of political rule over the "four quarters of the world," analogous to the North-South axis of the cosmos, can become a program for imperial expansion. The Christian differentiation of a "universal mankind under God" can be hypostatized into a quest for world empire. Voegelin writes that "[t]he possibility of making immanen-

---

[31] Eric Voegelin, *The Ecumenic Age*, p. 285.

[32] Ibid., p. 299.

tist nonsense of symbols which express the experience of divine presence in the order of man's existence in society and his-tory is always present."[33]

Derailment can take several forms. In the period of transition of classical philosophy to the speculation of the Stoics, philosophy was deformed into "doctrine." The symbols which Plato and Aristotle created to articulate their experience of reality evoked original experience of the world of existent things and transcendent reality that is not a god but the divine. But once philosophy ceases to be a medium of experience, Voegelin writes, "[a] new intellectual game with imaginary realities in an imaginary realm of thought, the game of propositional metaphysics, has been opened with world-historic consequences that reach into our own present."[34]

The Stoic dogmatization of philosophy, though destructive in its ultimate consequences, had the immediate effect of preserving the insight of classical philosophy against the inevitable defect that philosophy requires "philosophers" if it is to be preserved. In the absence of persons of the rank of Socrates, Plato, and Aristotle to continue the search for truth and of circumstances conducive to the contemplative life, the dogmatization of philosophy has at least preserved the symbols of philosophy. But the ravages of dogmatism can

---

[33] Ibid., p. 148.

[34] Ibid., p. 43.

be contained only so long before they take pernicious forms. For Voegelin, the concept of "ideology" represents the final turn in the decline of philosophy when the symbols no longer articulate original experience of theophany but become the means by which theophany is eradicated from public and personal consciousness.

Because the creation of ideologies historically occurs later, their construction includes a large arsenal of deformed symbols. For the symbol of the open soul, there is the symbol of the soul closed to divine reality. Voegelin calls this phenomenon "egophony," the creation of a system symbolic of the will of the system-builder to explain reality as a function of his own will. The experience of movement of the soul toward the divine becomes, in the work of modern "philosophies of history," the egophonous assertion that history culminates in one's own thought.

The Christian mystery of the Second Coming is deformed into egophonous certainty of a secular faith in the this-worldly success of the ideologist's own project for reconstituting reality. The political ideologies of the modern era are formidable, not the least because they are deformations of ontologically-oriented philosophic symbols of order. In this context, the attempt at recovering classic philosophy is a necessary first step in the recovery of personal and social order in the modern world.

Chapter 6

Arthur Finkelstein

On August 18, 2017, my friend Arthur J. Finkelstein died from lung cancer at his home in Ipswich, Massachusetts. For those who never met him, his obituary in the *Washington Post*[1] is as informative of Arthur's career and personal life as any. In January of that year, I had seen an encomium in *National Review* to Arthur, written by Reagan historian Craig Shirley, that looked like an obituary.[2] Arthur and I hadn't been in touch in quite awhile, so I sent him a message of my own expressing my admiration.

Arthur replied with one word, "Neat."

Arthur and I had been friends for more than forty-five years. That friendship began in 1972 when I joined the

---

[1] Matt Schudel, "Arthur Finkelstein, quietly influential GOP campaign mastermind, dies at 72," *Washington Post* (August 19, 2017) Available online through https://tinyurl.com/3wvccf9x

[2] Craig Shirley, "Not Just Good at National Politics, but the Best," *National Review* (January 26, 2017). Available online at https://www.nationalreview.com/2017/01/arthur-finkelstein-republican-political-consultant-strategit-conservative-libertarian/

faculty at the College of New Rochelle in New York as an Assistant Professor of Political Science. Arthur Finkelstein's office was up from New Rochelle on the Post Road in Rye, New York. We became friends, and I invited him to teach a course in campaign management in my department. In turn, he invited me to join a little political action group he had founded, the New York State Political Action Committee (PAC), where I became part of a group of Republicans. Among them were Priscilla Buckley and Carol Learsey, Bill Buckley's sisters, and Liz Doyle, a former member of the staff of *National Review*.

Arthur preferred PACs because donations were not limited. He was an early champion of Terry Dolan's National Conservative Political Action Committee (NCPAC). In fact, Terry Dolan gave Arthur and me a drive in his car after a meeting. That car represented the character of activist conservatives in the movement: old, cluttered with papers and debris, and unwashed. Dolan's life was politics, as was Arthur's.

Near Arthur's office in Rye was a Swiss restaurant called Gipfels, where I would meet him for meals. He graciously invited me and my wife to his home in Chappaqua. We were probably one of few so honored by this very private public man. I recall that once he drove me from a political meeting to my home in Tarrytown, NY, and told me that he was amazed that homes could still be bought for $75,000. By comparison, Arthur's home in Chappaqua, a converted barn, must have cost several hundred thousand dollars.

Arthur had an intuitive grasp of the nuances of American voters and was responsible for providing polling data that led to the election of James Buckley to the United States Senate. His career as a pollster was "world class," and a list of "his" candidates was surpassed only by the hilarious account of their eccentricities that Arthur would privately share.

But Arthur was also an unfailing observer not only of the mistakes of others, but also of his own. He was an inveterate gambler and aficionado of thoroughbred racing, and when on travel to Las Vegas would place a one hundred dollar bill in his shoe—just in case Lady Luck wasn't on the same trip.

Once, Arthur told me, he blew that hundred dollar bill and was broke. He picked up his phone at his hotel to make a call, and somehow another person was on the line. Arthur persuaded the caller on the crossed line to give him what he needed.

Campaigns run according to fixed schedules, and in off-years, Arthur's income was less than in years when he was involved in many campaigns. He persuaded me to try to get some government contracts for survey research. On our first try, we won a bid to survey the cost of government regulations for the U.S. Small Business Administration.

In one of the classes that Arthur taught at the College of New Rochelle, he challenged his students to give just one reason why they opposed the war in Vietnam. Arthur was an astute observer and knew that much of the opposition to that war was uninformed. But, on that day, a student raised her hand and said, "Mr. Finkelstein, I am opposed to the war because my brother was killed in Vietnam."

In my case, when in the first year of the Reagan Administration I was fired by Charles Z. Wick, Director of the United States Information and Communication Agency, from my presidential appointment as Director of Education and Cultural Affairs,[3] Arthur arranged for me to join the staff of Sen. Alfonse D'Amato. Arthur was responsible for Al D'Amato's election to the U.S. Senate, and in one meeting with Sen. D'Amato where Arthur was present, the topic of the right to abortion came up. I didn't share my opposition to abortion with the Senator, and Arthur took me aside and berated me. "You owe him," he said.

On two occasions, I tried to get Arthur to open up about his campaign work, first by encouraging him to write a book and on another occasion by asking him to do an online course. He didn't write the book, but he did give one lecture on campaign management that I recorded. An identical

---

[3] Richard Bishirjian, "Advice for Those With a Bad Boss: My Experience in the Reagan Administration" (March 11, 2018). Available online at https://theimaginativeconservative.org/2018/03/how-got-fired-reagan-white-house-richard-bishirjian.html

lecture given by Arthur on May 16, 2011, at the CEVRO Institute in Prague may be accessed at YouTube.[4]

The CEVRO Institute administrator who introduced Arthur gives a good summary of his career, including his work with Cliff White's "Draft Goldwater Committee," his work for Jesse Helms, and his work with Israel's Prime Minister Bibi Netanyahu. His relationship with Jesse Helms's Congressional Club led to his working on the campaign for a professor of political science in North Carolina, John East. Arthur decided immediately never to permit Professor East to be seen. East was a paraplegic confined to a wheelchair. Arthur also would not feature Alfonse D'Amato in campaign advertisements, preferring to feature D'Amato's mother. In New Hampshire, Gordon Humphrey, an airline pilot, was unknown. But Humphrey's wife sensed that Arthur knew something other consultants didn't. The Humphreys retained Arthur's services, and Gordon Humphrey won a campaign for the U.S. Senate.

I don't handle well the death of those I love, especially someone I would want to be my brother, and my learning of Arthur's death was no exception. Now, all I can do is include him in my list of friends—living and dead—for whom I pray nightly. I owe that to Arthur J. Finkelstein.

---

[4]https://youtu.be/IfCBpCBOECU

Chapter 7

John William Corrington

John William "Bill" Corrington lived an extraordinary life in which he mastered most of the instruments of Western intellectual culture to shape a political and legal philosophy, develop a philosophy of historical consciousness, compose works of literature and poetry of great beauty, and warn about the spiritual and social danger of the temptation for ersatz immortality of modern Gnosticism. That he made some money writing film scripts for Roger Corman or television scripts for a series produced by Procter & Gamble did not diminish his art.

In 1975, Bill Corrington published an essay entitled "Charles Reich and the Gnostic Vision."[1] The serial librarian at the College of New Rochelle saw this essay and brought it to my attention. That began a twelve-year friendship with Bill Corrington that lasted until his death on Thanksgiving Day, November 24, 1988.

---

[1] William Corrington, "Charles Reich and the Gnostic Vision," *New Orleans Review* 5, no 1 (1975).

My doctoral dissertation examined Gnostic aspects of the thought of Thomas Carlyle, and I published my findings in the *Journal of Politics*.[2] Carlyle, I demonstrated, was engaging in the actions of a Gnostic magician. Few colleagues then or today understood this line of argument, and I was delighted to make the acquaintance of Bill Corrington. He found Charles Reich to embody what Eric Voegelin called "modern Gnostic speculation."[3] On June 15, 1976, I wrote to Corrington expressing interest in his essay and a desire to "co-edit a work on modern Gnosticism." Two years later, that correspondence led to a conference entitled "Gnosticism and Modernity," conducted at Vanderbilt University on April 27–29, 1978.

Readers interested in literature and the cultural role of Southern literature will understand that Corrington experienced a clash between literature and philosophy. A defeated South lived in isolation from the nation at large for close to a hundred years after the Civil War. During that time, the politics of the South was dominated by the schemers, the corrupt, and the sociopaths. The South's intel-

---

[2] Richard Bishirjian, "Carlyle's Political Religion," *Journal of Politics* Vol. 38, no. 1 (February 1976): 95–113.

[3] Eric Voegelin, "The New Science of Politics," in *The Collected Works of Eric Voegelin*, vol. 5 (Columbia: University of Missouri Press, 2000), p. 192.

lectual elites retained their Southern character, and their integrity, by nourishing a unique Southern literature.

The *antebellum* South was dominated by social contract theories that justified slavery and, later, segregation of the races, believing that the nation was a confederation of states and that secession was permissible in a social contract.

With no avenue for true philosophy—other than that of John Locke—to develop in the South before the Civil War and with Southern society and commerce crippled for a hundred years thereafter, literature became the dominant expression of the deepest longings of Southern intellectuals for recovery of order. From that desire came a parade of great writers, poets, novelists, and professors of literature which culminated in what John Crowe Ransom's 1941 book *The New Criticism*.

John William Corrington was a child of that literary culture. He writes in his personal notebook:

It has been said that I am an apologist for the South. The South does not, and has never, needed an apologist... What my work really represents is the openness, the ambiguity, the vastness of the possibilities of human being in the mode of existence as it realizes itself in the

South in my time. Any work that deals with a certain place intensely is a celebration of that place.[4]

In a collection of Corrington's writings edited by Allen Mendenhall,[5] Mendenhall explains how he first encountered Corrington's work in a law school class, of all places, and situates Corrington's writings in reference to his life and times.

In a lecture that Corrington gave on the subject of writing, delivered in 1985 at the Northwest Louisiana Writer's Conference in Shreveport, Louisiana, Corrington told his audience that he knew very early that writing wouldn't make him wealthy, so he earned a Ph.D. in order to teach literature. He became department chairman of English at the Jesuit Loyola University of New Orleans, but by 1972 he left Loyola, angered by the University's treatment of a faculty member.

Corrington had had enough of Jesuit academia.

In the late sixties and early seventies, American higher education was unsuccessful in dealing with anti-Vietnam

---

[4] As quoted in Lloyd Halliburton, "The Man Who Slept with Women: John William Corrington's *Shad Sentell*," *Legal Studies Forum* 27 (2003): 664.

[5] Allen Mendenhall, *The Southern Philosopher: Collected Essays of John William Corrington* (University of North Georgia Press, 2017), ix-xvii.

war protesters who, in their wisdom, claimed that serious subjects, seriously taught, were "irrelevant." In response, the Ivy League gutted its curriculum, faculty engaged in "teach-ins" and spouted Marxist-Leninist slogans, and university administrators sat quietly while protestors held them captive in their offices. There occurred a concerted effort to crush the academic freedom of anyone whose opinions differed from those of the mob or their college-administrator accessories who aided and abetted the rioters.

Mendenhall has collected other essays, including a lecture that Corrington delivered in 1966 as part of a discussion series created by the National Defense Education Act. There, Corrington discusses reality and illusion and the writer's use of common speech to communicate that experience.[6]

Another early essay, "A Poet's Credo" (1966), expresses his frustration with academic journals:

So now the battle lines are shaking themselves into recognizable shape: we can play the sewaneeatlantic-kenyonhudsonpartisan2 game, or we can play for keepsies and hold onto our nuts.[7]

---

[6] Ibid., p. 24-29.

[7] Ibid., p. 35.

This sentence captures both the robust humor that makes Corrington's writing style refreshingly uncommon and the frustration he felt with the commerce of literature.

A lecture that Corrington delivered to the South-Central Modern Language Association in 1971 that criticizes "message literature," or what we today would call "PC," or "political correctness," reveals Corrington's disgust with the corruption of writing that was so prevalent as America was recovering from the excesses of the 1960s.[8] One wonders if he was ever invited back to any meetings of the MLA.

Bill Corrington remained a Southern writer of literature but, one day, he was ruminating among the bookshelves in the library at Tulane University. In frustration with academic politics, he had given up college teaching at Loyola-New Orleans and was studying law at Tulane. Ever inquisitive, Corrington found volume one of Eric Voegelin's *Order and History*, entitled *Israel and Revelation*. When he returned home, as I mentioned in Chapter 5, he informed his wife, "By God, he's done it." What "it" was doesn't need explaining. Corrington discovered that Voegelin had recovered the philosophical mode for examining the experience of what every Southern Baptist, Methodist, or Church of Christ believer knows—that God intervenes in history.

---

[8] Ibid., p. 51-53.

The American nation that Bill Corrington experienced upon reaching maturity had long before begun the journey away from Western Christianity. In the modern era, that can be traced to the spiritual injury done to Americans by our Civil War (and a long series of wars into the twenty-first century that America has endured and sometimes welcomed) and the acceptance of Darwin's *On the Origin of Species* (1859) that turned the hearts and minds of post-Civil War Americans toward science and against the Protestant Christianity that dominated American culture at the time.

As explained in Fr. James T. Burtchaell, III, CSC's study of America's religious colleges, those that had been solidly Christian became secular in a generational "dying of the light."[9] And, of course, that turning away had deep roots in the Enlightenment philosophy that inspired the framing of the Constitution of the United States and, particularly, the Declaration of Independence of Thomas Jefferson.

"Reason" and "science," as understood in the restricted sense that those concepts have in modern culture, outline the origins of the cultural, intellectual, and "religious" disorder of our times. I place the word "religious" in quotation marks because religion, as Wilfred Cantwell Smith observed, is

---

[9] James T. Burtchaell, *The Dying of the Light: The Disengagement of Colleges and Universities from their Christian Churches* (Grand Rapids, MI: Eerdmans, 1998).

different from "faith."[10] The passion for religion reflects the perspective of an observer. Faith reflects experience of transcendent divine reality. Bill Corrington, by this meaning, was "faithful."[11]

Corrington's study of philosophy in light of the work of Eric Voegelin created a chasm between him and the Southern literary critics who taught literature in such places as Vanderbilt, the University of South Carolina, and the University of Dallas. In that respect, he was like Flannery O'Connor and Marion Montgomery, who pursued the study and writing of literature from the perspective of Voegelin's recovery of classical philosophy.[12]

Mendenhall has collected all of Corrington's works that reflect that "leap in being,"[13] to use a concept from Voegelin, that describes the transformative experience of the ancient

---

[10] Wilfred Cantwell Smith, *Faith and Belief: The Difference between Them* (Oxford: Oneworld Publications, 1998) and Wilfred Cantwell Smith, *The Meaning and End of Religion* (New York: New American Library, 1962).

[11] His dying words were, "It's alright."

[12] See Marion Montgomery, "The Poet and the Disquieting Shadow of Being: Flannery O'Connor's Voegelinian Dimension," *Intercollegiate Review* 13 (Fall 1977): 3–14

[13] Thomas Hollweck, "Cosmos and the 'Leap in Being' in Voegelin's Philosophy," paper presented at the Eric Voegelin Society meeting, Washington, DC, 2010. Available online at https://papers.ssrn.com/sol3/papers.cfm?abstract_id=1666989

Greek philosophers who transcended cosmological myth. After making that leap, Corrington was so out of place among "academic" teachers of Southern literature that, like Socrates, who became ill when he left Athens, he became refractory when he encountered English teachers.[14]

The seminal essay in this collection that reveals what Corrington achieved in breaking away from literature as an academic enterprise and entering into the interpretation of literature as an act of philosophy is his 1986 lecture given at Kansas State University. In that lecture, Corrington interprets a passage from an early essay by T. S. Eliot:

> . . . the whole of the literature of Europe from Homer and within it the whole of the literature of [one's] own country has a simultaneous existence and composes a simultaneous order.[15]

That "order," Corrington writes, exists concretely in the psyche of the poet who experiences something that Heraclitus called the *zynon,* "that which is common to all," in which time is lost in the fathomless reaches of that psyche

---

[14] Corrington told me that he was rejected for a position in the English department at the University of Dallas because during his visit he "cursed."

[15] Allen Mendenhall quoting from T.S. Eliot's "Tradition and the Individual Talent" in *The Southern Philosopher*, p. 89.

whose limit, Heraclitus tells us, cannot be plumbed, so deep is its Logos.[16]

Anyone who has studied Voegelin understands that this is the *arche*, the beginning in the West of a unique Western philosophic mode of existence in which the philosopher interprets the human psyche "as the instrument for experiencing transcendence."[17] Influenced by Voegelin, Corrington was now beginning to read literature from the perspective of the soul's response to the divine ground of being. Corrington writes, "the great driving force at the foundation of human culture ... is the human *psyche* in search of itself in the multiplicity of its forms, dimensions, and possibilities—and the loving and fearing tension within that *psyche* toward the divine ground."[18]

Because that drama of the soul is the ontological basis of all literature, not only the literature of the West, Corrington is critical of Eliot for confining his essay to "half a hemisphere," leaving out Asia and India. It is in Eliot's poetry, and the footnotes in Eliot's "The Wasteland," however, that Corrington finds the range of historical materials that informed Eliot's art and those "notes explode the idea of an

---

[16] Ibid., p. 90.

[17] Voegelin, "New Science of Politics," p. 141.

[18] Voegelin to Bishirjian, October 21, 2016, in the author's possession.

ideal order comprised exclusively of European literary monuments."[19]

Bill Corrington knew he was playing with fire since the literary critics who made Southern literature famous belonged to what Voegelin called "a mutual admiration society."[20] They relished the particular, the regional, even the noncommercial character of Southern society. They especially wanted to read texts closely and not prejudge them with theories. Like Presbyterian churches that have only one bathroom, these Southern literary critics read literature only one way.

I can explain this a bit better by reference to a meeting of The Philadelphia Society in New Orleans on October 13, 1979, where the topic was "The South and American Conservatism."[21] Andrew Lytle, a Southern Agrarian writer, dramatist, and professor of literature, gave a presentation on a presumed golden age of the "Southern Agrarians." During the discussion period, I confronted Lytle with the observation that growing up in Pittsburgh, I experienced loyalties to neighborhood, church, family, the Pirates baseball team, and the Pittsburgh Steelers that were equivalent to growing up in the agrarian South. He did not agree. Lytle, and so

---

[19] Ibid., p. 98.

[20] Conversation with Eric Voegelin at the University of Dallas, 1971.

[21] http://phillysoc.org/meetings/past-meetings.

many other Southerners, believed that the world of the South
was *the* world.

Bill Corrington and I finally met in person to discuss a
possible volume entitled "Gnosticism and Modernity," and
that led to an invitation on September 1, 1976, to Eric
Voegelin. Voegelin responded on September 6:

> . . . when I hit on this problem, that was 25 years ago. In
> the meanwhile, science in this matter has advanced. And
> today I would have to say that Gnosticism is one com-
> ponent in the historical structure of modernity but no
> more than one. Of equal importance, it has turned out,
> are Apocalyptic, Neoplatonism, Hermeticism, Alchemy,
> and Magic.[22]

Corrington commented on Voegelin's explanation in a
letter dated September 30, 1976:

> If I were to define Gnosticism as widely as Voegelin
> does—including Hegel and Marx in it—it should be no
> problem to subsume these other symbolisms also. I
> would hope that new investigations & findings will not
> tend to create semantic battles in an area which has not
> yet made nearly enough penetration into political

---

[22] Eric Voegelin to Richard Bishirjian, September 6, 1976, in
the author's possession.

science as a theoretical tool to afford quibblers as to what is Gnosticism, what is Hermeticism, & so on.[23]

Voegelin followed up in a letter dated October 21, 1976:

The literature on Magic, Neoplatonism, Apocalyptic, Kabbalah, Hermeticism, and Alchemy is growing prodigiously and can be read by anybody who cares to read it. All of these are components in the present intellectual disorder, just as is Gnosticism. On one special point, not treated sufficiently elsewhere, I have dwelled in my *Ecumenic Age*, that is on the transformation of mythical and revelatory symbols into "doctrines."[24]

By December 20, 1976, Corrington and I agreed that we would first hold a symposium on the theme "Gnosticism and Modernity." In a joint letter mailed to prospective participants, we wrote:

---

[23] Corrington to Bishirjian, September 30, 1976, in the author's possession. The "quibblers" were those, the letter added, who "walked away from Voegelin's first formulation of modernity as Gnostic. It was, simply, too political, for German Voegelinians escaping political reality in political theory."

[24] Voegelin to Bishirjian, October 21, 2016, in the author's possession.

The term "Gnosticism" should be understood, we feel, in an extended rather than in a narrow sense. Generally, we take our inspiration from the work of Professor Eric Voegelin whose use of the concept in its generic sense includes those intellectual movements such as Hermeticism, Alchemy, Magic, Kabbalah, Rosicrucian[ism], Millennialism, and certain strands of Neoplatonism and Scientism. Obviously, we are concerned with patterns of "Second Reality," using Musil's phrase, which tend to contract consciousness of reality.[25]

An undated, handwritten letter accompanies the abstract of Corrington's paper entitled, "Gnosticism and Modern Thought: A Way You'll Never Be." Voegelin was impressed and called it "the best paper" in a symposium that he said "was the best I have attended." The text of that paper is found in part four of Mendenhall's volume.[26]

The final version of the paper prepared for publication is entitled "The Structure of Gnostic Consciousness" and is a *tour de force* in which Corrington reaches into his past as a novelist, calling up the "mythical structure" on which great literature depends. Corrington argues that the Gnostic personality "is unable to maintain the balance in tension" of existence and to "seek release from the disorder and con-

---

[25] Allen Mendenhall, *The Southern Philosopher*, p. 270.
[26] Ibid., p. 157-203.

fusion it experiences. . . . The result is a speculative return from the noetic field . . . to the mythopoetic field."[27]

Corrington's sensitivity to mythic imagination enables him to understand that some who cannot traverse the distance between myth and philosophy may choose to return to myth and the control that choice allows. "Such people choose, in Professor Voegelin's phrase, to live in a certain untruth rather than in an uncertain truth."[28]

Corrington concludes that all classical Gnostic speculation is but "a regression to an archaic mythopoetic mode of thinking in which Gnostic manipulative magic is possible. [This] reversal constitutes fantasy-construction of the first order."[29]

There are political conclusions that we can infer from Corrington's paper and from his critique of Charles Reich as Gnostic. Corrington understood that the world in which he lived was a dangerous place because so many persons were living in a fantasy world of their own construction, and the most dangerous of them wanted to compel him to join them in their world. If he did not obey them, they would kill him.

---

[27] Ibid., p. 145.

[28] Ibid., p. 146.

[29] Ibid., p. 149.

Chapter 8

Paul Weyrich

I knew Paul Weyrich from the founding of the Free Congress Foundation in 1974 and recall being with him and James Whelan about the time that Whelan became the first editor of the *Washington Times* in 1982, a publication owned by the Korean spiritual leader, the Rev. Sun Myung Moon. I was responsible for preparing Whelan's book entitled *Allende, Death of a Marxist Dream* for publication by Arlington House in 1981.

As a student at the University of Wisconsin, Paul Weyrich was active in the Young Republicans and the Goldwater campaign. He then became a newspaper reporter and radio and television commentator in Wisconsin. From there he moved to Colorado where he became news director for KQXI, the Arvada, Colorado AM radio station. Coincidentally, KQXI's offices on University Boulevard were six and a half miles distant from the offices of Yorktown University, which I had founded in Denver.

In 1966, Paul Weyrich became press secretary to Republican Senator Gordon Allott, and through his work for a U.S. Senator in Colorado, Weyrich became friends with Joseph

Coors and members of the Coors family. Joe Coors was impressed with Weyrich's strategy for recovery of the conservative movement after Watergate and bankrolled Weyrich's cofounding of The Heritage Foundation with Edwin Feulner and in 1974 his founding of the Committee for the Survival of a Free Congress.

"Free Congress," as it came to be known, played a role in defeating many Liberal Democrats Senators who were elected in the wake of the Watergate scandal. And in an encomium to Paul Weyrich at his death, Morton Blackwell, president of The Leadership Institute, wrote,

> Beginning in the early 1970s, conservatism was on the march. The election of Ronald Reagan in 1980 constituted a major triumph for conservative principles. ... And none of it would have happened without Paul Weyrich. If there had been no Paul Weyrich, there would, in all likelihood, have been no Heritage Foundation. And had there been no Heritage Foundation—and the many other new and improved conservative organizations Paul created or made possible—Ronald Reagan would not have been elected in 1980.

Morton Blackwell cited a list of conservative organizations that Paul Weyrich founded or was one of the key people in starting:

Heritage Foundation

Free Congress Foundation

Free Congress PAC

Coalitions for America

House Republican Study Committee

Senate Steering Committee

Council for National Policy

International Policy Forum

American Legislative Exchange Council

American Association of State and Local Officials

Conservative Leadership PAC

Paul was a committed Catholic, but after Vatican II he joined the Melkite Greek Catholic Church where he served as a deacon. Feeling that Christian political conservatives had retreated from politics after the humiliating loss of Barry Goldwater in 1964 and the disappointing performance of the Nixon Administration (1969-1974), Weyrich worked with the Rev. Jerry Falwell in 1979 to found what they called the "Moral Majority."

Four years later, in 1983, I formed the World News Institute with Daniel W. Johnson, a college classmate from the University of Pittsburgh. Dan had been station manager of "Pitt's" campus radio station, became station manager of a Chicago television station, and then formed DWJ Associates, a public relations agency that used a news format to promote businesses and politicians. With Dan's production people, I conducted a field survey of Israel and its Muslim neighbors for a video we produced for distribution on television. Dan Johnson understood the coming force of cable television, and I told Paul Weyrich about this new type of cable media. Weyrich, in 1993, founded National Empowerment Television (NET), a cable network designed to mobilize the Religious Right. At one stage, NET claimed to reach more than 11 million homes. Paul attributed his decision to found NET to my influence.

In February, 1999, Paul outlined in a public letter a strategy for Christians to become engaged in politics even though they have been defeated in some elections and disappointed in many politicians whom they supported:

> I believe that we probably have lost the culture war. That doesn't mean the war is not going to continue, and that it isn't going to be fought on other fronts. But in terms of society in general, we have lost. This is why, even when we win in politics, our victories fail to translate into the kind of policies we believe are important.
>
> Therefore, what seems to me a legitimate strategy for us to follow is to look at ways to separate ourselves from the institutions that have been captured by the ideology of Political Correctness, or by other enemies of our traditional culture.
>
> What I mean by separation is, for example, what the homeschoolers have done. Faced with public school sys-

tems that no longer educate but instead "condition" students with the attitudes demanded by Political Correctness, they have seceded. They have separated themselves from public schools and have created new institutions, new schools, in their homes.

I think that we have to look at a whole series of possibilities for bypassing the institutions that are controlled by the enemy. If we expend our energies on fighting on the "turf" they already control, we will probably not accomplish what we hope, and we may spend ourselves to the point of exhaustion.

In December, 1999, I visited Paul to tell him that I was going to start a solely Internet university committed to teaching the principles, philosophy, theology, and literature of Western civilization. Paul assisted by providing me the database of his donors and became a member of the Board of Directors of what became known as Yorktown University.

Paul and I got along probably because we came out of the same university environment in the 1960s, and we worked on Barry Goldwater's 1964 campaign for president. Though I am anticlerical with a grave distrust of Catholic priests, some popes, and many Protestant ministers and the Protestant denominations they serve, I attended many weekly luncheons that Paul held for his religious bedfellows whom he encouraged to become active in politics and more sophisticated in their understanding of spiritual disorders affecting American society and culture.

Several members of Yorktown's board of Trustees that included Paul Weyrich, Gilbert Davis, Louis Barnett, Victor Milione, and me.

Perhaps most indicative of Weyrich's understanding of the importance of ideas was his identification of "Political Correctness" with "Cultural Marxism" as the spiritual disorder of the late 20th century. His sponsorship of William Lind's analysis and explanation of Cultural Marxism to political organizations throughout America was typical of Paul Weyrich's leadership.[1] Analysis of this ideology developed

---

[1] "The Origins of Political Correctness," *Accuracy in Academia*, February 5, 2000. https://www.academia.org/the-

by the Frankfort School associated with the Institute for
Social Research at Goethe University in Frankfurt, Germany,
was not typical of "conservative" Think Tanks and that was
why "Free Congress" and Paul Weyrich ennobled all who
came to know him.

---

origins-of-political-correctness. Also see this video lecture:
http://kitmantv.blogspot.com/2009/07/history-of-political-
correctness.html

Chapter 9

Arthur Laffer

Every political conservative in America was and is committed to free markets, but for decades Republicans railed against deficits. Once elected they would raise taxes in order to reduce deficits and then were defeated for reelection. Not trained as an economist, my knowledge was limited to a summer course at Grove City College on economics taught by Hans Sennholz and my reading of Frederick Hayek's *Road to Serfdom*. I knew something about the marginal theory of labor of the Austrian School and taught a two semester course on Communist Ideology. I can claim to have read Marx's book on Capitalism. But an economist, I was not.

I experienced a lesson on Supply-side Economics when Howard Jarvis utilized California's initiative process, established in 1911, by which voters are given power to enact legislation. In 1978, "Prop 13" amended the Constitution of California by placing a ceiling on valuation of property taxes. Proposition 13 limited tax increases to 1% of the purchase price of property. Supply-side Economics is the economic theory behind limiting tax increases.

The School of Supply-side Economics was represented by economists Robert Mundell, Arthur Laffer, Norman Ture, Allan Reynolds, and members of the professional staff of the U.S. House of Representatives and Senate including Richard Rahn, Paul Craig Roberts, Bruce Bartlett, and members of Congress, Jack Kemp (R-NY), and William Steiger (R-WI). They were assisted by Bob Bartley and Jude Wanniski at the *Wall Street Journal*.

The supply-siders offered a counter to the demand orientation of John Maynard Keynes. Keynes's idea of the managed state offered a revolutionary perspective that quickly dominated economic thought when first propounded in two books: *The Economic Consequences of the Peace (1919)* and *General Theory of Employment, Interest and Money (1936).*[1]

John Maynard Keynes's political economy was based on the assumption that limits on government supported by the 19th-century free market theories of classical liberalism were simply inadequate to modern conditions.

Keynes was an advocate for empowering national government with "new managerial duties" to supplant free exchange of goods and limited state power with "a system of capitalism in which large business, not for profits and the

---

[1] James Piereson, *Shattered Consensus: The Rise and Decline of America's Postwar Political Order* (New York: Encounter Books, 2015).

government operated to promote the public interest."[2] Diminished in influence, if not superseded by the state, were the unfettered actions of "banks, the wealthy and investment houses."[3]

Piereson observes that to accomplish this, Keynes rejected "three postulates of classical economics."

1) Say's Law, which holds that supply creates demand;
2) Widespread unemployment as a consequence of business cycles;
3) The practice of "saving," which Keynes considered to be "leakage" from demand or withdrawal of consumption.[4]

Prosperity lay in consumption and debt, not in thrift and saving.

Those assumptions were present in a second stage of the New Deal programs of President Franklin D. Roosevelt, called the "Second New Deal," that made significant changes in the administration and to the purpose of the American economy. For political conservatives who came of age with the growth of the conservative movement, the great bane of our lives were New Deal programs and agencies that limited

---

[2] Ibid., pp. 22-23.

[3] Ibid, p. 25.

[4] Ibid., p. 31.

our ability to save for retirement and whose popularity led to new government programs and agencies proposed by Democrats and Republicans alike.

Finally, however, we were given a well thought out justification for lowering taxes. In the second year of my organizing an Internet university, I asked for a meeting with economist Arthur Laffer.

I met Art Laffer in the offices of Laffer Associates in Del Mar, California, and Laffer expressed his willingness to create a course on Supply-side Economics thus returning to public life after retreating from public commentary when Chilean secret agents attacked his compound.

Laffer was an advocate of the policies of Chilean president Augusto Pinochet from 1973 to 1981. Pinochet replaced radical Marxist minority President of Chile, Salvador Allende, who was killed in a coup attempt by dissident right-wing Chileans. Pinochet introduced policies designed to recover from the destruction of the Chilean economy by seeking counsel of what was known as the Chicago School of Economics. Art Laffer taught in the University of Chicago business school at the same time that Milton Friedman presided over the Economics Department.

Prominent among the Chicago School economists are Gary Becker, Ronald Coase, Milton Friedman, Friedrich Hayek, Frank Knight, and George Stigler. Stigler was Art Laffer's dissertation director.

Art Laffer and others gave counsel to Pinochet, and Laffer published frequent commentaries about the application of Supply-side principles in Chile. The Chilean secret police are known for assassinating opponents of the Chilean regime, and some dissident members who were opposed to Pinochet decided to take out Art Laffer.

Laffer's multi-acre family estate in Delmar contained Art Laffer's home, a conference center for clients of Laffer Associates, and a game park replete with exotic animals. Agents from Chile entered the compound, slaughtered a horse, and left the horse's head at Laffer's front door. Efforts made by the U.S. Secret Service and local police to apprehend the perpetrators came to nothing, so security of his compound was improved by a wire fence and lighting that illuminated the grounds. A second successful attack was made, and another slaughtered animal placed at Laffer's doorstep. Laffer took the only action that was available to him and withdrew from public life.

In late 2001, he told me that he was now willing to "go public" and do a course on Supply-side Economics for my Internet university. Unfortunately, I was ahead of myself. I did not learn how to develop effective online courses for another eight years and knew nothing about economics. So, Arthur Laffer's course never made it into our curriculum.

I was frustrated, and Art Laffer was disappointed, but he graciously invited me to one of his conferences at his conference center. In 2009, we awarded him an honorary degree.

I presented the degree at his office in Tennessee where he
had moved his company because of lower taxes in that state.

Though I failed Art Laffer, I promoted Supply-side Economics at two events at FreedomFest, a salon-like encounter
with the best and brightest minds, and recorded lectures by
Richard Rahn, Steve Entin, Mark Skousen, Allan Reynolds,
and Steve Moore. Art Laffer gave a graduation speech.

Here is the text of Art Laffer's Honorary Degree:

> In our great democracy where everyone is equal,
> "Greatness," "Leadership," and "Historic" are three
> words that may not be equally applied, nor are they often
> used to describe one man. Yet those words describe the
> gifts, ability and spirit of Arthur B. Laffer.
>
> Yorktown University believes that Arthur Laffer
> earned those accolades the hard way, and in doing so he
> paid a price in Academe and in his personal life for his
> commitment to principle. For those principles, Arthur
> Laffer willingly endured the disdain of Keynesian Eco-
> nomists, aspiring Presidents of the United States who
> described Supply-side Economics as "Voodoo," assorted
> politicians of both parties, and incumbent Presidents of
> the United States who derided Supply-side tax cuts as
> "trickle down" economics. Nevertheless, Arthur Laffer
> persisted in his commitment to the principle so that all
> Americans would enjoy the benefits of economic growth
> and prosperity.

In honor of that leadership, Yorktown University's Faculty and Board of Trustees desire to honor Arthur Laffer with a Master of Arts in Government and Political Economy *honoris causa*. As we enter an era of less prosperity, higher taxation, and government's seizure of a greater share of Gross Domestic Product, it is well and good to honor Arthur Laffer in this way.

The work in Economics conducted by Arthur Laffer, and his personal commitment to the principles of what came to be called Supply-side Economics, influenced public finance in the United States. His efforts in Georgia, California, Arizona, and dozens of other states where he found openness to Supply-side economic policies has made him an influence for the good throughout the fifty United States. As an adviser to Prime Minister Margaret Thatcher during the 1980s, he certified the international consequences of the Supply-side movement, and his service to President Ronald Reagan is an important chapter in American presidential history.

Dr. Laffer is welcomed into the Yorktown University community of scholars for his B.A. in economics from Yale University and M.B.A. and Ph.D. in economics from Stanford University. Those earned academic degrees commenced Arthur Laffer's lifelong commitment to higher education. Dr. Laffer was a Distinguished University Professor at Pepperdine University and a member of the Pepperdine Board of Directors and a Founding Director of Yorktown University. He also held the Charles B. Thornton chair in Business Economics at the University of Southern California, and he was an Associate Professor of Business Economics at the University of Chicago and a member of the University of Chicago faculty from 1967 through 1976. This honorary degree honors those real academic achievements, his impact on American public policy, and his contribution to decades of economic growth that would not have occurred had Arthur Laffer chosen an easier path.

Only in 2015, however, did we develop a course on Supply-side Economics with Raymond Keating. Here is a list of topics from that course:

1. The principles of Supply-side Economics and how they can be traced to the English moral philosopher, Adam Smith, and the French Economist, Jean-Baptiste Say.

2. How Mark Skousen's original lecture on Say's Law defines the foundations of Supply-side Economics.

3. How President Woodrow Wilson's successors, Presidents Warren Harding and Calvin Coolidge, re-

versed President Wilson's policies, spurred economic growth, and started "the Roaring Twenties."

4. Amity Shlaes's discussion of the economic policies of President Calvin Coolidge.

5. How the tax policies of Presidents Harding and Coolidge were destroyed by the return to high tax-and-spend policies of President Franklin Roosevelt's New Deal.

6. Why President John F. Kennedy's Supply-side tax cuts were cut short by the tax and spend policies of President Lyndon Johnson.

7. The actual recording and transcript of President John F. Kennedy's Supply-side speech.

8. Why Art Laffer calls President Lyndon Johnson's successors, Presidents Richard Nixon, Gerald Ford, and Jimmy Carter "the three Stooges."

9. A commencement address by Dr. Art Laffer.

10. What happened when Supply-side policies were widely publicized by Bob Bartley and Jude Wanniski at *The Wall Street Journal*.

11. Economist Richard Rahn's moving commemoration of the achievement of Jack Kemp.

12. How President Ronald Reagan's acceptance of tax reform from anti-tax activist Howard Jarvis led to a Supply-side "Revolution."

13. Listen to Steve Entin and Alan Reynolds give original lectures on the Reagan tax cuts.

14. Sad but true! After President Reagan: Supply-Side opposition grew in the United States, but Reagan's policies are adopted in more than 50 countries.

15. Econ101 concludes with an examination of the economic policies of President William Jefferson Clinton and two Yale-educated Presidents, George H. W. Bush and George W. Bush.

Chapter 10

Angelo Codevilla

In September, 1965, Gerhart Niemeyer, Professor of Government at the University of Notre Dame, mentioned to me that a new graduate student from Rutgers University in New Jersey had arrived and that I had seen him the day before as Niemeyer and he had passed me walking on campus.

I told Niemeyer that the person that was walking beside him couldn't be the same person. "The person you were with was a European."

That young graduate student was Angelo Maria Codevilla.

Codevilla was, like me, a Goldwater conservative and was attracted to Notre Dame because he had been introduced to the university by Richard V. Allen at an Intercollegiate Studies Institute (ISI) Summer School in 1963. Fr. Stanley Parry, CSC, and Professor Gerhart Niemeyer were both a great influence on Richard Allen.

Another graduate student, Robert McDonough, was a political conservative who had taken some courses from

Willmoore Kendall. Kendall had also taught Fr. Parry when Fr. Parry was a graduate student at Yale.

In addition to Codevilla, McDonough, and me, two others, namely Howard Segermark, a Catholic graduate of John Carroll University, and William Gangi, a very conservative student of Con Law from St. John's College in Queens, New York, made up a core group of five graduate students who would later contribute ideas to a growing conservative movement.

We five politically-conscious conservatives in the Graduate School of Government class of '64-'65 were the ingredients of an identifiable "brand" of conservatives who sought graduate degrees from Notre Dame immediately after the '64 Presidential election.

If the Department Chairman, Fr. Stanley Parry, CSC, had been drinking less and not facing a mid-life crisis questioning his having become a Catholic priest, the Department would have been filled with "Goldwater conservative" graduate students.

The five of us who did enroll got there on our own, not because we were recruited.

Two other distinctly different types of graduate students were graduates of Assumption College in Worcester, Mass. At that time, classes at Assumption were taught in French, and two of our fellow students, Patrick Powers and William Murphy, were the epitome of what we understand as an

American "Catholic" intellectual with continental French views and values.

In our own way, we five Goldwater conservatives, like the Assumptionists of 19th-century France, had reacted negatively to the secularization of America that was apparent in the 1960s, the difference being that I was a Missouri Synod Lutheran and Angelo Codevilla was an Italian from Italy with typical Italian attitudes toward the "-ism" of "Catholicism"—and a Lutheran.

Our professors, Niemeyer and Voegelin, were not Catholics and were not Thomists. In other words, the graduate school where we were students was the opposite of what most Catholic Americans thought a Catholic institution was and should be. The religious order that had founded the University of Notre Dame had become very much a post-Vatican II institution: Notre Dame's "Catholicism" was theologically and politically "Liberal," directed at achieving "Social Justice" and idolizing President John F. Kennedy.

This was the University of Notre Dame led by Fr. Theodore Hesburgh, CSC, better known for its football team. Codevilla, McDonough, Gangi, Segermark, and I liked "the fighting Irish" and its head coach, Ara Parseghian, but we would have none of that "JFK idolatry," and each of us would act as a corrective to '60s Liberalism of those times throughout our professional careers. But let me permit Dr. Codevilla to tell his story.

I arrived in America at age thirteen in 1956 without knowledge of English but with an excellent Italian education that put me ahead of my American cohort. I also came with some set attitudes: a disposition to love America, commitment to academic excellence, anti-communism (my gang used to fight a gang of commie kids, and our family—which worshiped work—despised the commies as lazy and violent.)

Like many Lombards, I was a devout Christian but aggressively anti-clerical. The Lutheran pastor next to whom we lived had no trouble convincing me that Luther was more Catholic than the Pope.

By 1958, after "Sputnik," Fort Lee High School decided to graduate me in three years instead of four because of my love for and performance in Physics.

In 1960, by the time I started Rutgers at age seventeen, I had become an American and picked up the standard American bad habits—plus the disastrous impression that, always having gotten "A's" and praise without working, I could continue to do so. I learned otherwise the hard way. After graduation from high school, I worked as a Chemistry lab assistant for a year while going to college at night, and returned to Rutgers in 1962 having lost my lust for lab work and picked up the notion that I should be a diplomat.

I fell in love with French literature, took political science courses and quickly gained contempt for political science and its "Professor" with whom I very much loved arguing.

At Rutgers I met "Jim," whose last name I have forgotten, who headed the local Conservative Club, affiliated with ISI. Jim had no more trouble taking me in than the Lutheran pastor had.

In February 1963, I met Ann. Everything I've done and not done ever since has flowed from my love of her. God may punish me for violating the First Commandment.

In April 1963, I took up an invitation from ISI to attend a conference in Philadelphia on U.S./ Soviet relations, featuring all manner of eminent scholars. Harvard's Robert Osgood stood out. But to me he sounded as stupid as my poli sci Profs. So, I stood up and asked a series of questions that reduced him to babble, and the audience began cheering me on. Thereafter, another participant in the ISI seminar, Dick Allen, introduced himself. We talked at length and then [he] took me to lunch with Robert Strauz-Hupé and Eleanor Lansing Dulles, sister of John Foster Dulles and Allen Dulles. I kept in touch with Dick Allen who [had] talked to me about Gerhart Niemeyer. I had read Niemeyer in ISI pamphlets, but

Dick Allen told me of the intellectual windows Niemeyer could open for me.

In 1963 and 1964—very political years—I naturally campaigned for Goldwater on campus and as part of the NJ Young Republicans. Our gang delighted in rising up against and defeating the Rockefeller forces.

At the time, my major intellectual influence was Clarence Turner, professor of Romance Languages at Rutgers, who had studied with the great Charles Hall Grandgent in the 1910s, and from whom I took a memorable course on Dante and another almost as memorable on Montaigne—all in the original, with 5 students in each class.

In 1964-1965, my academic attention was diminished because Ann had been shipped off to Berlin. I managed to get to Europe and spirit her off to Italy.

I went to Notre Dame on scholarship in September 1965 where I never worked harder than I did for Niemeyer. His course on Modern Political Ideology remains a pillar of my mind. But South Bend is 753 miles from New Brunswick, which is where Ann was doing her senior year. So, after 3+ weeks of work, I would get into the car on Thursday at 4:00 am and arrive in time to meet her as she got out of class at 3:15. I would return the following Monday. This occa-

sioned the following conversation, repeated to me by
Dick Bishirjian.

Niemeyer: Vere is mister Codevilla.
Bishirjian: He's in New York, Prof. Niemeyer
Niemeyer: Und vot is he doing in New York?
Bishirjian: His girlfriend is there.

This is an accurate account, except for the German accent of our professor whom Angelo Codevilla memorialized in a May 2013 essay entitled "Thank you, Gerhart Niemeyer."[1]

Leaving undergraduate or graduate school—even briefly—during the Vietnam War placed you at risk to "the Draft." When I left Notre Dame to study Latin at Loyola of Chicago and classical Greek at Hunter College, I had to stay in those programs or be shipped off to Boot Camp and a land war in Asia. With his future wife, Ann, more than 700 miles distant in New Jersey, South Bend, Indiana was not the place Codevilla wanted to be. Leaving the graduate program at Notre Dame put him at risk, however, and he was drafted!

I shall pick up this "Ennobling Encounter" with Dr. Angelo Codevilla by reference to an interview that he gave to

---

[1] Angelo Codevilla, "Thank you, Gerhart Niemeyer," *University Bookman* (May 5, 2013). https://kirkcenter.org/best/thank-you-gerhart-niemeyer

David Samuels at "The Tablet"[2] and share my encounter
with him by reference to some of his important and influential books and essays.

David Samuels writes of being "an attentive reader of
Codevilla's book *Informing Statecraft*, which together with
Norman Mailer's novel *Harlot's Ghost* offers a fair guide to
the karmic evolution of the U.S. intelligence community."
The interview is worth reading because it reveals Codevilla's
deeply rooted commitments and his willingness to offend,
even David Samuels.

One of Codevilla's commitments is to "meritocracy" by
which persons are advanced based on merit, not whom you
know or your parentage. Gifted in mastery of language
(Italian, French, English), Codevilla "tests well" and when
given the opportunity to advance by testing he is at the "top
of his class."

Drafted after leaving Notre Dame, Codevilla became a
naval officer and tested upward into the ranks of the foreign
service. Sheer ability enabled Codevilla to serve as an intelligence specialist under Malcolm Wallace (R-WY), for whom
he served on the professional staff of the U.S. Senate's Select
Committee on Intelligence. Serving as Sen. Wallace's designee saved him from being removed from the Committee's

---

[2] David Samuels, "The Codevilla Tapes," *The Tablet* (October
24, 2019).

staff by Sen. Barry Goldwater who fired him only to have him
reinstated within a day.

To David Samuels, Codevilla comments on merit and
how what he calls the Ruling Class subverts advancement on
merit:

> In living memory, and I'm an example of that, it was
> for a time possible for nonliberal Democrats to get into
> the American foreign service, and if they did as I did, and
> scored number one in their class, they would have their
> choice of assignments. But now, you have all sorts of new
> criteria for admission into the foreign service, which
> have supposedly ensured greater diversity. In fact, what
> they had done was to eliminate the possibility that the
> joint might be invaded by lesser beings of superior intel-
> ligence.

Another of Codevilla's commitments that he reveals to
David Samuels is his commitment to limited government
and anger that the Constitution has been subverted by the
growth of an administrative state:

> You are describing, and the textbooks describe, what
> used to be the American system of government, which
> has not existed since the late 1930s. The last attempt to
> revive that system, to make it rise up out of the overlay
> of administrative agencies that the New Deal built, was

the Supreme Court of *Schechter Poultry vs. the United States*, 1935, the essence of which decision was to say that a legislative power cannot be delegated. Were that maxim to be enforced, the FAA, the FCC, and on and on, all of these agencies would cease to exist because they are, quite literally, unconstitutional. Now the Supreme Court has held them to be constitutional under the fiction that they are in fact merely filling in the interstices of laws.

However, your average law passed by Congress these days consists almost exclusively of grants to these agencies to do whatever it is they wish.

Codevilla's fascination with higher education's connection to the Ruling Class is also revealed:

the defining feature of the ruling class is a certain attitude. And that attitude developed in the academy, and that attitude became uniform throughout the country because of the uniform academy. The uniformity of the academy transformed itself into the uniformity of the ruling class.

Though his reputation as a political philosopher commands our attention, he is the author of several studies on U.S. Intelligence and a critic of the U.S. Central Intelligence Agency. Two studies were published under the auspices of the National Strategy Information Center. NSIC was led by

Frank Barnett, who favored tough-minded experts in such fields as U.S. national security policy, strategic studies, Soviet studies, and arms control.[3] Angelo Codevilla was one of Barnett's "tough-minded experts." Underlying his studies of "Intelligence," though, is his awareness of the intelligence community's prejudices:

> [A] whole bunch of prejudices.
>
> So, the straightforward political prejudices are, in no particular order: liberalism, prejudice in favor of the Arabs. You probably are not aware of the corporate prejudices that existed in the favor of the Soviet Union. And they were very, very powerful at CIA, as opposed to DIA or NSA.

In an essay Codevilla published in *The Tablet* for March 24, 2021, entitled "American Exodus,"[4] he expresses his disdain for "Cancel Culture."

---

[3] Jeffrey H. Michaels, "Waging 'Protracted Conflict' Behind the Scenes: The Cold War Activism of Frank R. Barnett," *Cold War Studies*, Vol. 19, Issue 1 (Winter 2017).

[4] Angelo M. Codevilla, "American Exodus," *The Tablet* (March 24, 2021). Available online https://www.tabletmag.com/sections/news/articles/american-exodus-angelo-codevilla-oligarchy

[I]solating and alienating anybody, let alone half the country, is the proverbial two-edged sword. Anytime you isolate and alienate someone else, you do the same to yourself. The boundaries that the oligarchs have drawn, are drawing, separate them from the American people's vast majority, whose consciousness of powerlessness and defenselessness clarifies their choice between utter subjection and doing whatever it might take to exit a system that no longer seems to allow for the prospect of republican self-government.

On education he observes:

[T]he schools are teaching their children less than they had been taught. They have been mortgaging the house to pay for college. Their children's student loans mortgage their future. But the colleges have produced mostly worthless degrees while credentialing a generation of oligarchs who pretend to control other people's lives.

Around the country, Americans are fleeing public K-12 schools as fast as they can. This exodus accelerated during the COVID affair as parents observed online the poor quality if not outright dysfunctionality of much that the schools teach. The teachers' unions stimulated it by showing their priority for their material and ideological interests. Only because most Smiths don't have the resources for private education or for home schooling is that exodus not accelerating faster.

Simply "search" for the name "Angelo Codevilla" at *Law & Liberty,* the *American Spectator,* the *Claremont Review of Books,* the *Hoover Institute Working Group on Military History, National Review,* the *Washington Times* and *American Greatness,* and you will appreciate why I am ennobled by his friendship.

In order to get to the pinnacle of his successful career, Codevilla had to leave Lombard, Italy, at a young age and emigrate to "the New World." If you've been to Milan, Italy, you can appreciate the difference between Milanese and southern Italians. As a colleague once remarked, "Codevilla is a Goth." Indeed, Codevilla is as tall as I imagine some Goths were, much like Alaric who was compelled by invading Normans to abandon his traditional homeland and invade Rome.

Codevilla's fluent Italian, French, and English assured his growth as a scholar and point to a serious deficiency in American higher education that can be traced to our isolation from non-English speaking cultures and especially to the limits of the American system of "public" education. Into this cauldron of declining culture, Codevilla quickly sized up what was happening and, like a good Goth, began to attack!

Codevilla attacks the stupid, incompetent, self-serving, and delusional among us, but not with abandon. In each phase of his career: a) as an intelligence authority and during service on the Congressional staff of the Select Committee on Intelligence, b) as a member of the professional staff at the Hoover Institution, c) as a professor of International Relations at Boston University, and d) as an essayist on every area of professional expertise he has mastered, Codevilla conveys fear and admiration.

So great was the Central Intelligence Agency's fear of his criticism that the CIA gave a one million dollar "grant" to stop publication of Codevilla's last volume on the CIA's intelligence failures. That view of CIA incompetence and bureaucratic self-interest is expressed in Codevilla's review of two books about the CIA where he writes:

Former CIA Director "George Tenet's *At the Center of the Storm* and John Prados's *Safe for Democracy* show, each in its own way, that the CIA serves not the national interest of the United States but its own corporate interests and its partisan vision. It will continue to do so until a president who understands this remakes U.S. intelligence from the ground up." [5]

---

[5] "Intelligence Failures," *Claremont Review of Books,* Vol. VII, Number 3 (Summer 2007). Available online at https://claremontreviewofbooks.com/intelligence-failures/

The elite journal *The Atlantic* also came under criticism in an essay entitled "The Ever Shallower Atlantic."[6] One need not ask what *The Atlantic*'s Editor in chief, Jeffery Goldburg, thought when he read that "*The Atlantic*, treats ordinary Americans' religiosity as a problem, and calls all who do not share its worldview racist, sexist, homophobic, any affected by whatever psychosocial disease the class happens to in-vent."

How must Arthur Schlessinger, Jr., have felt when Codevilla referred to Schlessinger's *War and the American Presidency* that historian Robert Dallek called "a book for all seasons… an American classic" as "a sad indication of how partisanship has crushed academic standards."[7]

Of our professional bureaucrats at the U.S. Department of Defense, Codevilla asks, "How and why have latter-day American statesmen and soldiers so fouled the relationship between military means and political ends that … they have managed to lose wars despite winning battles?"[8]

---

[6] Angelo M. Codevilla, "The Ever Shallower Atlantic," *Claremont Review of Books* (Oct 24, 2016). Available online https://claremontreviewofbooks.com/digital/the-ever-shallower-atlantic/

[7] Angelo M. Codevilla, "Soldiers, Statemen, and Victory," *Claremont Review of Books,* Vol. III, Number 2 (Spring 2003). Available online https://claremontreviewofbooks.com/soldiers-statesmen-and-victory/

[8] Ibid.

Of Codevilla's many books, I will comment on three:

1. *Putting America First: John Quincy Adams's Teachings for Our Time*[9]
2. *The Ruling Class: How They Corrupted America and What We Can Do About It*[10]
3. *To Make and Keep Peace Among Ourselves and with All Nations*[11]

Codevilla's *Putting America First* is an encomium to John Quincy Adam's political realism:

> Adams believed, practically even more than theoretically, that governments behave as they think suits them at any given time whether or not a treaty exists to enjoin or to forbid. The reality of will, of agreement or disagreement, supersedes documents. Hence, Adams's

---

[9] Angelo M. Codevilla, *Putting America First: John Quincy Adams's Teachings for Our Time* (Washington, DC: Republic Book Publishers, 2021).

[10] Angelo M. Codevilla, *The Ruling Class: How They Corrupted America and What We Can Do About It* (New York: Beaufort Books, 2010).

[11] Angelo M. Codevilla, *To Make and Keep Peace Among Ourselves and with All Nations* (Palo Alto, CA: Hoover Institution Press, 2014).

diplomacy was about clearly, carefully, defining all sides' interests, aiming less at treaties than at maximizing real, reciprocal, understanding and forbearance.

Maintaining and developing the American people's independent, peculiar, way of life, and its national interests is the paramount objective of all foreign policy.

For foreign relations, that paramountcy means that the U.S has no substantive objective regarding foreign countries—none. Only the avoidance of trouble with them. Hence, following George Washington's injunction, peace must be America's objective with all nations —interfering with none, brooking no interference from any. Even in commercial relations, America is to "force nothing," to seek no special advantages, nor to wage economic warfare. Reciprocity is to be U.S. foreign policy's end as well as its means.

Codevilla writes that Adams was guided by the following realities:

1) The American people, by the very right by which they asserted their independence are bound to respect that of others. "Who has appointed us judges in their case?"

2) "Their business" their quarrels, their objectives really are their own, beyond the American people's right or

powers to shape them. By taking sides in foreign interests we lose sight of our own.

3) At the very least, such involvement raises the possibility of wars that are of tangential interest to us – sure to kill some Americans, but unlikely to realize any American's dreams. ...

4) America is solely sovereign over its own business – peacefully and securely to occupy its natural borders, and within them to show of what virtue and of what manner of perfection "free men and Christians" are capable. Focusing on that business means first, as Washington had prescribed, growing America's power.

And here is the nub of Codevilla's admiration of John Quincy Adams:

Prior to Progressivism, labeling any proposal or point of view as "America first" would have been meaningless. Statesmen had debated policy within their fiduciary responsibilities' natural focus: America itself.

But since the Progressives' paramount premise is precisely that U.S policy's proper primary concern must be with mankind as a whole, and with America only incidentally and derivatively, the label "America first" became an imputation of narrow-mindedness, selfishness; in short, of illegitimacy.

In 1939-41, FDR used it to smear calls for armed neutrality as pro Nazi.

This observation brings my attention to the context in which Codevilla wrote *The Ruling Class*. In the interview with David Samuels that Codevilla gave to *The Tablet*, he observes,

[T]here is no such thing as America anymore. In place of the America that is described in history books has arisen something new and vast and yet distinctly un-American that for lack of a better term is often called the American Empire...the Democrats were the senior partners in the ruling class. The Republicans are the junior partners.[12]

Published in 2010, *The Ruling Class: How They Corrupted America and What We Can Do About It* contains an introduction by Rush Limbaugh. As Limbaugh explains, he saw Codevilla's essay on this topic in *The American Spectator* and devoted an entire program to reading passages for his audience.[13]

---

[12] David Samuels, "The Codevilla Tapes," *The Tablet* (October 24, 2019). Available online at https://www.tabletmag.com/sections/arts-letters/articles/angelo-codevilla

[13] Ibid., p. ix-x.

Few scholars of Classical political philosophy achieve celebrity by endorsement of a dominant Talk Radio host. Codevilla did not go out of his way to become famous. He just attacked in the 20th century AD as a Goth like Alaric attacked in the 5th century AD. That's what Goths do best.

The Ruling Class is an indictment of an oligarchy constituting itself as "Rulers" of others who, though of equal citizenship, pray to God and whose lives may be characterized by devotion to "marriage, children, and religious practice." Believed by the Ruling Class to be less intelligent, these others are the target of a campaign to reduce "American families intellectual and moral subordination to science." Published in 2010 before the Coronavirus pandemic released feelings of negativity toward "experts" whose expertise gives them unelected power to restrict the lives of the great majority, a target of Codevilla are these very "experts" who confuse their own opinion with "science." This Ruling Class has undermined marriage and has taken "as much authority from parents as it can."

Lest we miss what Codevilla intends, early in the introductory pages he proposes that "doing away with the Ruling Class' power and perquisites is the prerequisite for saving America's prosperity, civility and morality."[14] America's rulers have become "a self-contained, self-reverential class." Both "Republican and Democratic office-holders ... share a

---

[14] Ibid., p. xxi.

similar presumption: to dominate. . . . They think, look, and act as a class, almost a caste."[15]

Codevilla asks, "How did America change from a place where people could expect to live without bowing to privileged classes?"[16] Once upon a time, "America's upper crust was a mixture ... who were not predictably of one mind on any given matter." Back then, our schools and universities "had not imposed a single orthodoxy about the origins of man, about American history, or about how America should be governed."[17] Our "Founding Fathers" believed in equality due to an understanding that "all men are made in the image and likeness of God" because they yearned for equal treatment under British rule or "because they had read John Locke."[18]

The Progressives rejected that and held that man is "a mere part of evolutionary nature."[19] Their belief in "progress" gave the early Ruling Class an expectation of peaceful change (under their direction). Today's Ruling Class, however, is arrogant and condemns what Codevilla calls "the Country Class." Obama apologized for America's failing to meet its responsibilities. Clinton apologized to Africans for

---

[15] Ibid., p. 3.

[16] Ibid., p. 8.

[17] Ibid., pp. 8-9.

[18] Ibid., p. 16.

[19] Ibid., p. 17.

slavery in America, and George H.W. Bush told Gorbachev that Reaganites are "dummies and blockheads."[20]

Is there a solution by which "to untangle such a corrupt knot?" Yes, Codevilla believes, "only by mobilizing ... on a principled moral basis ... being willing to dispense with whatever threads of it they hold."[21] It won't be easy, but by taking up the responsibilities of citizens, fathers, and entrepreneurs, the Ruling Class can be deposed.[22] At issue is whether the Country Class is "willing to shoulder the responsibilities that their grandparents bore as proud badges of American citizenship."[23]

The answer that Codevilla gives to that question is unfurled in his 2014 study that examines the tenuous existence of domestic and international peace in our time. Published by Hoover Institution Press, with a "Foreword" by Victor Davis Hanson, Codevilla's *To Make and Keep Peace Among Ourselves and with All Nations* makes the observation that since 1914 war has been absent "only during two brief periods (1919-41, 1992-2001)."[24]

---

[20] Ibid., pp. 24-25.

[21] Ibid., p. 69

[22] Ibid., p. 81

[23] Ibid., p. 85.

[24] Angelo M. Codevilla, *To Make and Keep Peace Among Ourselves and with All Nations* (Palo Alto: Hoover Institution Press, 2014), xvii.

We Americans have come to terms with the absence of peace, yet our living life on a war footing is not what the generation that founded the American nation intended.

Codevilla enshrines with high praise the two leaders who sought peace and gave us advice for the avoidance of war: George Washington and John Quincy Adams.

And Codevilla observes that the two documents on which we should rely if we desire peace are Washington's "Farewell Address" of 1796 and the Declaration of Independence which, for Adams, was pivotal to the enjoyment of peace with other nations and to shaping the character of the American people.

In Adam's address on July 4, 1821, he explained why:

America, in the assembly of nations, since her admission among them, has invariably, though often fruitlessly, held forth to them the hand of honest friendship, of equal freedom, of generous reciprocity. She has uniformly spoken among them, though often to heedless and often to disdainful ears, the language of equal liberty, equal justice, and equal rights. She has, in the lapse of nearly half a century, without a single exception, respected the independence of other nations, while asserting and maintaining her own. She has abstained from interference in the concerns of others, even when the conflict has been for principles to which she clings, as to the last vital drop that visits the heart.

Abstaining "from interference in the concerns of others" was the "Great Rule" asserted by George Washington in his "Farewell."

> . . . in extending our commercial relations to have with them as little political connection as possible. . .even our Commercial Policy should hold an equal and impartial hand neither seeking nor granting exclusive favours or preferences; consulting the natural course of things; diffusing & diversifying by gentle means the streams of Commerce, but forcing nothing.[25]

Over the course of the book, Codevilla traces how American presidents and statesmen have ignored President Washington and in doing so adversely affected the moral and spiritual character of the American nation.

That, I believe, explains the spirit that moves Codevilla throughout his career: Codevilla is a moralist.

So much harm experienced by the American nation could have been avoided if these later writers and statesmen had heeded President George Washington's "Great Rule": Josiah Strong, Albert Beveridge, Theodore Roosevelt, Walt Whitman, Nicholas Murray Butler, David Starr Jordan, Woodrow Wilson, Elihu Root, Andrew Carnegie, and William Howard Taft.

---

[25] Ibid., 7.

It is beneficial to remember the names of these men because from 1885 to 1929, Codevilla writes, they reshaped the character of Americans by habituating them to trans-mutation of "pertinent questions into meaningless general-ities."[26] Some examples from my list include the following:

Josiah Strong's *Our Country: Its possible future and its present crisis* (1885) is "permeated by the sense that the United States is God's and Darwin's designee 'for perfection and domination of the planet.'"[27]

Senator Albert Beveridge (R-IN), an imperialist, said in a speech in the U.S. Senate on January 9, 1900, that "self-government and internal development have been the dominant notes of our first century; administration and the development of other lands will be the dominant notes of our second century."[28]

Codevilla questions the idea that "[t]o impose American rule on others is not to deny them liberty, because we know what liberty is, and they do not. Does imposition violate something fundamental about America? No: 'The Declara-tion of Independence does not forbid us to do our part in the re-generation of the world. If it did, the Declaration would

---

[26] Ibid., p. 125.

[27] Ibid., p. 90.

[28] Ibid., p. 93.

be wrong.' So much for piety toward America's foundations."[29]

Nicholas Murray Butler, president of Columbia University, and advocate of disarmament. In 1907, Butler wrote "All navies are a bane on the world. And it is high time that the United States . . . reduce its naval building program." [30]

David Starr Jordan, president of Stanford University, proposed "eugenically refining the American people to lead the world."[31]

Woodrow Wilson "had replaced the compass of concrete peace with a utopian creed."[32] And was "always just one enemy's elimination away from perpetual peace."[33]

Elihu Root supported acquisition of the Philippines as a way "America could show the world a new kind of stewardship." [34] He also advocated for international organizations to

---

[29] Ibid., p. 93.
[30] Ibid., p. 101.
[31] Ibid., p. 102.
[32] Ibid., p. 118.
[33] Ibid., p. 103.
[34] Ibid., p. 99.

settle disputes. Root won a Nobel Prize for founding the International Court of Justice.

William Howard Taft presided at a convention on June 17, 1915, to form a "League to Enforce Peace," an organization that foreshadowed Woodrow Wilson's League of Nations.[35] Joining Taft at Independence Hall were Elihu Root, Alexander Graham Bell, Rabbi Stephen S. Wise, James Cardinal Gibbons of Baltimore, and Edward Filene on behalf of the recently founded U.S. Chamber of Commerce. Elected to the Executive Committee were Harvard President Abbott Lawrence Lowell, former Cabinet member and diplomat Oscar S. Straus, and Henry Holt, publisher of *The Independent*, an anti-slavery paper, and president of Rollins College.

What can explain this change in principles governing American statecraft a mere century and a third after President Washington warned against foreign entanglements?

I believe there were three influences: a savage American Civil War, Darwin's *Origins of the Species,* and the import of German idealism by the Transcendentalists. Americans had exchanged the God of Christianity with a new faith in man's

---

[35] Ibid., p. 107.

divinity. A belief that man is divine appealed to these powerful men who constituted a "clerisy or power."[36]

If they thought their legacy was a world at peace, however, they did not reckon on an ideology like Marxism-Leninism that would overthrow the Russian monarchy and seek world dominion. How "the West" responded to this ideology of Revolution was complicated by the overthrow of Habsburg Germany and the Ottoman Empire while a savage war was being waged in France. An empowered Soviet Union controlled Eastern Europe, the ideology of Mao took control of China, and a Great Depression led the American President Franklin Delano Roosevelt to reconstitute the American government into an administrative state.

Before the Great Depression in 1929 and President Franklin Roosevelt's election in 1932, America was a world of individual freedom protected by voluntary associations, churches, rights of citizenship, and the rule of law which gave hope for a better life for the vast majority of Americans. A European war from 1914-1918 was fatal to European civilization because it transferred morals and religion to "the nation-state." The transfer of allegiance from civil society to the State were not felt in America for a decade.

Before that change in grounding occurred, it was furrowed by disconnecting the means of defending peace to

---

[36] Richard Bishirjian, *The Conservative Rebellion* (South Bend, IN: St. Augustine's Press, 2015), p. 89.

enthusiasm for a "utopian creed."[37] Strong, Wilson, and the distinguished statesmen in their train of followers had divested America of its capacity to protect the peace.[38] In turn, America's character "as defined by the Declaration of Independence," as John Quincy Adams had believed, was altered.[39]

Adam's July 4, 1821, address articulates the connection between the Declaration and the character of the American nation.

> From the day of the Declaration, the people of the North American union, and of its constituent states, were associated bodies of civilized men and Christians, in a state of nature, but not of anarchy. They were bound by the laws of God, which they all, and by the laws of the gospel, which they nearly all, acknowledged as the rules of their conduct. They were bound by the principles which they themselves had proclaimed in the declaration. They were bound by all those tender and endearing sympathies, the absence of which, in the British government and nation, toward them, was the primary cause of the distressing conflict in which they had been precipi-

---

[37] Codevilla, *To Make and Keep Peace Among Ourselves and with All Nations*, p. 118.

[38] Ibid., p. 109.

[39] Ibid., p. 70.

tated by the head-long rashness and unfeeling insolence of their oppressors. They were bound by all the beneficent laws and institutions, which their forefathers had brought with them from their mother country, not as servitudes but as rights. They were bound by habits of hardy industry, by frugal and hospitable manners, by the general sentiments of social equality, by pure and virtuous morals; and lastly they were bound by the grappling-hooks of common suffering under the scourge of oppression. Where then, among such a people, were the materials for anarchy!

The apparatus of the administrative state and a national security establishment that was housed in "that deep State" had eradicated American *"habits of hardy industry, by frugal and hospitable manners."* Since 1885, a "pseudo technical fog" was developed that has clouded judgment by making it amoral to counter the dogma that reduced thinking to a choice between total peace or annihilation of nuclear war.[40]

---

[40] Ibid., p. 131.

About the Author

Richard J. Bishirjian is the founder the American Academy of Distance Learning, Inc. He earned a B.A. from the University of Pittsburgh and a Ph.D. in Government and International Studies from the University of Notre Dame.

Dr. Bishirjian was Gerhart Niemeyer's teaching assistant at Notre Dame. He was an assistant professor in the Department of Politics at the University of Dallas in Texas, chairman of the Political Science Department at the College of New Rochelle in New York, and founder of Yorktown University, where he served as President and Professor of government from 2000-2016.

He served as a political appointee in the Reagan Administration and in the administration of George H. W. Bush.

He is the editor of *A Public Philosophy Reader* and author of three books: *The Development of Political Theory, The Conservative Rebellion,* and *The Coming Death and Future Resurrection of American Higher Education.* His most recent work, *Coda,* is a novel published by En Route Books and Media. His three most recent scholarly studies are *Ennobling Encounters, Rise and Fall of the American Empire,* and *Conscience and Power.*

Dr. Bishirjian's essays have been published in *Forbes, The Political Science Reviewer, Modern Age, Review of Politics,*

Chronicles, the *American Spectator* and *The Imaginative Conservative.*

Books, Essays, and Reviews

Publications by Dr. Richard Bishirjian

Book: *Ennobling Encounters* (En Route Books and Media, August 2021).
https://enroutebooksandmedia.com/ennoblingencounters/

Novel: *Coda* (En Route Books and Media, August 2020).
https://enroutebooksandmedia.com/coda/

Book: *Rise and Fall of the American Empire* (Completion Date: November 2021).
http://www.academydl.com/rise-and-fall-of-the-american-empire/

Book: *Conscience and Power* (Completion Date: November 2021).
http://www.academydl.com/conscience-and-power-2/

Essay: "Prelude to Civil War: Francis Graham Wilson on Spain," in *Modern Age* (Spring 2019, pp. 36-41).
https://isi.org/modern-age/prelude-to-civil-war-francis-graham-wilson-on-spain/

Review: "Harry Jaffa, Walter Berns and American Conservatism," by Steven Hayward in *The Imaginative Conservative* (Nov 5, 2017). http://www.theimaginativeconservative.org/2017/11/patriot ism-is-not-enough-steven-hayward-richard-j-bishirjian.html

Review: *The Southern Philosopher: Collected Essays of John William Corrington* by Allen Mendenhall, *Anamnesis* (September 2017). *Anamnesis* has ceased publication. http://anamnesisjournal.com/2017/09/realitys-defender/

Book: *The Coming Death and Future Resurrection of American Higher Education* (St. Augustine's Press, 2017). http://www.staugustine.net/our-books/books/the-coming-death-and-future-resurrection-of-american-higher-education-1885-2017/

Book: *The Conservative Rebellion* (St. Augustine's Press, 2015). http://www.amazon.com/Conservative-Rebellion-Richard-Bishirjian-Ph-D/dp/1587311585/

Essay: "Dreams versus Reality," *Chronicles* (July 13, 2015). https://www.chroniclesmagazine.org/dreams-vs-reality

Essay: "Grammy Anarchy," *Chronicles* (February 11, 2015). https://www.chroniclesmagazine.org/grammy-anarchy/

Essay: "Origins and End of the New World Order," *Modern Age* (Summer 2014), pp. 195-209.
https://isi.org/modern-age/origins-and-end-of-the-new-world-order/

Essay: "MOOCs versus HCOCS," National Association of Scholars (July 16, 2014).
https://www.nas.org/articles/moocs_vs._hcocs_higher_cost_online_courses

Essay: "Leo Strauss and the American Political Religion," Modern Age, Fall 2014, pp. 7-18.
https://isi.org/modern-age/leo-strauss-and-the-american-political-religion/

Essay: "Preparing the Scapegoats for Slaughter," The Martin Center (July 30, 2010).
https://www.jamesgmartin.center/2010/07/preparing-the-scapegoats-for-slaughter/

Review: "The Death of Conservatism" by Sam Tanenhaus in *Modern Age*, Vol. 52, No.3 (Summer, 2010), pp. 243-245.

Essay: "Quantification and Intelligence Testing," *Humanitas*, Vol. 22, Nos. 1 & 2 (2009), pp. 185-192.
http://www.nhinet.org/bishirjian22-1.pdf

Essay: "Difficult Labor: The Perils of Birthing a New College," *Academic Questions*, Vol. 22, No. 3 (Summer 2009), pp. 284-297.
http://link.springer.com/article/10.1007%2Fs12129-009-9115-9#/page-1

Essay: "The Federal Takeover of Higher Education," The James Martin Center (March 6, 2007).
https://www.jamesgmartin.center/2007/03/the-federal-takeover-of-higher-education/

Essay: "Why I am a conservative," *Modern Age*, Vol. 49 (Summer 2007), pp. 200-204.
https://isi.org/modern-age/why-i-am-a-conservative-symposium/

Essay: "The United States in the World Arena," *Modern Age* (Winter 2007), pp.86-90.
https://isi.org/modern-age/the-united-states-in-the-world-arena-two-opposing-views/

Monograph: *The American Political Tradition and the Nature of Public Philosophy*, Copley Custom Publishing, Acton, MA, 2004. Second printing 2006.

Essay: "Online Stock Offerings are Overregulated," Forbes.com, March 2001.

Review: "The Politics of Truth and Other Untimely Essays: The Crisis of Civic Consciousness" by Ellis Sandoz, *The Review of Politics*. Vol. 62. No. 1. Christianity and Politics: Millennial Issue II (Winter 2000), pp. 181-184.

Article: "The Creation of a Conservative Intellectual: 1960-65," in *Modern Age* (Winter, 1998). https://isi.org/modern-age/i-the-creation-of-a-conservative-intellectual-1960-1965/

Article: "Daimonic Men," in *Modern Age* (Winter, 1996), pp. 162-166.

Article: "Hegel and Classical Philosophy," in *Modern Age*, Vol. 35, No. 2 (Winter, 1992), pp. 126-134. https://isi.org/modern-age/hegel-and-classical-philosophy/

Review: Aftersight and Foresight: Selected Essays by Gerhart Niemeyer in University Bookman, Volume 29, Number 3, 1989, pp. 4-8.

Article: "The Problem of Carlyle's Religion," in *The Good Man in Society: Active Contemplation*, Gueguen, Henry & Rhodes, eds. (Lanham, MD: University Press of America, 1989), pp. 75-90.

Monograph: *The Nature of Public Philosophy* (Lanham, MD: University Press of America, 1982).

Article: "Civil Religion and American Foreign Policy" in The Hillsdale Review (Spring, 1981), Vol. III, No. 1, pp. 3-11.

Review: Eric Voegelin, *Anamnesis* [English translation] in *Christianity and Literature*, vol. xxvii, no. 4 (Summer, 1979), pp. 76-79.

Article: "Wilson, Croly and the American Civil Religion," in *Modern Age*, Vol. 23, No. 1 (Winter, 1979), pp. 33-38.

Review: Dale Vree, "On Synthesizing Marxism and Christianity" in *The Academic Reviewer* (Winter, 1979), pp. 27-28.

Review: James Robinson, ed., The Nag Hammadi Library in English, in *Christianity and Literature*, Vol. xxvii, no. 3 (Spring, 1979), pp. 77-78.

Book: *A Public Philosophy Reader*, ed, with an introductory essay (New Rochelle: Arlington House Publishers, 1978).

Book: *The Development of Political Theory: A Critical Analysis* (Dallas: The Society for the Study of Traditional Culture, 1978).

Review: "Bernard Crick, Political Theory and Practice" in *Modern Age* Vol. 22, No. 1 (Winter 1978), pp. 94-96.

Review: Robert Nisbet, "Sociology as an Art Form" in *New Oxford Review*, Vol. XLV, No. 1 (January 1978), pp. 20-21.

Review: Michael Novak, "The Joy of Sports" in *The Academic Reviewer* (Spring/Summer 1978), pp. 1-2.

Article: "The Public Philosophy in American Democracy," in *The Intercollegiate Review*, Vol. 13, No. 2 (Winter/Spring 1978), pp. 95-100.

Review: Robert Nisbet, "Twilight of Authority" in *New Oxford Review* (March 1977), pp. 19-20.

Review: Thomas Molnar, "Authority and Its Enemies" in *Modern Age,* Vol. 21, No. 3 (Summer 1977), pp. 318-19.

Review: Sebastiano Timpanaro, "On Materialism" in *The Journal of Politics*, Vol. 39, No. 2 (May 1977), p. 548.

Article: "Carlyle's Political Religion," *The Journal of Politics*, Vol. 38, No. 1 (February 1976), pp. 95-113. http://www.journals.uchicago.edu/doi/abs/10.2307/212896 3

Review: Bernard Crick, "In Defense of Politics" in *The Occasional Review*, Issue 5 (Autumn 1976), pp. 123-127.

Review: Thomas Molnar, "God and the Knowledge of Reality" in *The Alternative* (June/July, 1975), pp. 30-31.

Article: "Thomas Hill Green's Political Philosophy," in *The Political Science Reviewer*, Vol. 4 (Fall 1974), pp. 29-53.

Review: George Anastaplo, "The Constitutionalist: Notes on the First Amendment" in *Modern Age*, Vol. 17. No. 1 (Winter 1973), pp. 93-94.
https://isistatic.org/journal-
archive/ma/17_01/bishirjian.pdf

Contact Dr. Bishirjian by e-mail at academydl@gmail.com to schedule him to speak to your group.

Made in the USA
Monee, IL
05 September 2021